SUCCESS WITHOUT COLLEGE

Careers in Sports, Fitness, and Recreation

Robert F. Wilson

BARRON'S

All inquiries should be addressed to:
Barron's Educational Series, Inc.
250 Wireless Boulevard
Hauppauge, New York 11788
http://www.barronseduc.com

International Standard Book No. 0-7641-1562-6

Library of Congress Catalog Card No. 00-068014

Library of Congress Cataloging-in-Publication Data

Wilson, Robert F.
　　Careers in sports, fitness, and recreation / Robert F. Wilson.
　　　　p.　cm.—(Success without college)
　　Includes bibliographical references and index.
　　ISBN 0-7641-1562-6 (alk. paper)
　　1. Sports—Vocational guidance.　2. Physical education and training—Vocational guidance.　3. Recreation—Vocational guidance.　4. High school graduates—Vocational guidance.　I. Title.　II. Series.
　　GV734.3 .W55 2001
　　790'.023'73—dc21

00-068014

Printed in Hong Kong

9　8　7　6　5　4　3　2　1

Table of Contents

TABLE OF CONTENTS

Careers in Sports, Fitness, and Recreation

You can earn a living doing what you *like* to do.

Enjoying your work—what a concept! Yet this is not only possible, but with thorough planning and hard work, not really difficult to accomplish.

Let's say you are a high school student, or recent graduate, with an interest in one or more sports, or one or more fitness or recreation activities. You can't decide what to do with your life because no traditional career options interest you—not those you have thought about on your own, nor those your parents or guidance counselors have suggested to you. You've decided not to go to college for now, for financial reasons, because you have no idea what you'd specialize in, or because right now it just seems like a waste of time.

Why not try to make that sports, fitness, or recreation interest work for you? You won't necessarily get to the top of any of these professions without additional education or training—often both. But you can get access to one or more of them, and while you're at it find out if you'd really like to be in that particular field before you invest a lot of years and money finding out.

Tens of thousands of young men and women are working in jobs they never thought they could have. As fitness instructors, personal trainers, snowboard repairers, or fishing guides, they opted out of factory work and found a way to fill their days with work they enjoyed doing. Sometimes there was a false step or two along the way, and maybe this will be true for you, as well. We've included the stories of some of these successful people in this book, many of whom started out just about where you are right now. Through these stories you'll be able to look at some of the jobs in depth, and follow the career paths of the professionals who hold these jobs. We'll also show you:

- how to compete successfully for the job you want

- what the job you're after is really like, and what it takes to do it well

- what your chances are for success, both professional and financial.

All of the men and women profiled on the following pages enjoy professional success today at least in part because they followed solid job-search strategy. All have pursued their career goals both rigorously and systematically. *Success Without College: Careers in Sports, Fitness, and Recreation* passes on to you some of the strategies that have worked for them. For example, it will help you:

- determine both an immediate and long-range career path

- prepare a marketing strategy to get you there

- write a résumé and cover letters that best communicate your specific job qualifications

- sharpen your interviewing skills to improve your chances of getting a job offer

- keep a checklist on your next job to track all changes as your career goals change.

Many of the occupations covered in this book have been projected by the *Occupational Outlook Handbook* (developed by the U.S. Department of Labor's Bureau of Labor Statistics) to grow either *faster* than average between now and 2008—by which they mean an employment increase of from 21 to 35 percent—or *much faster* than average during that period, or an employment increase of 36 percent or more. The market potential for most of the sports, fitness, and recreation jobs described on the following pages, in other words, is excellent.

So use the tools described in the book; take as much time as you need to decide which career to pursue, then go after it as hard as you can. Good luck, and let us know how you're doing from time to time.

Robert F. Wilson
bobwilson@job-bridge.com
www.job-bridge.com

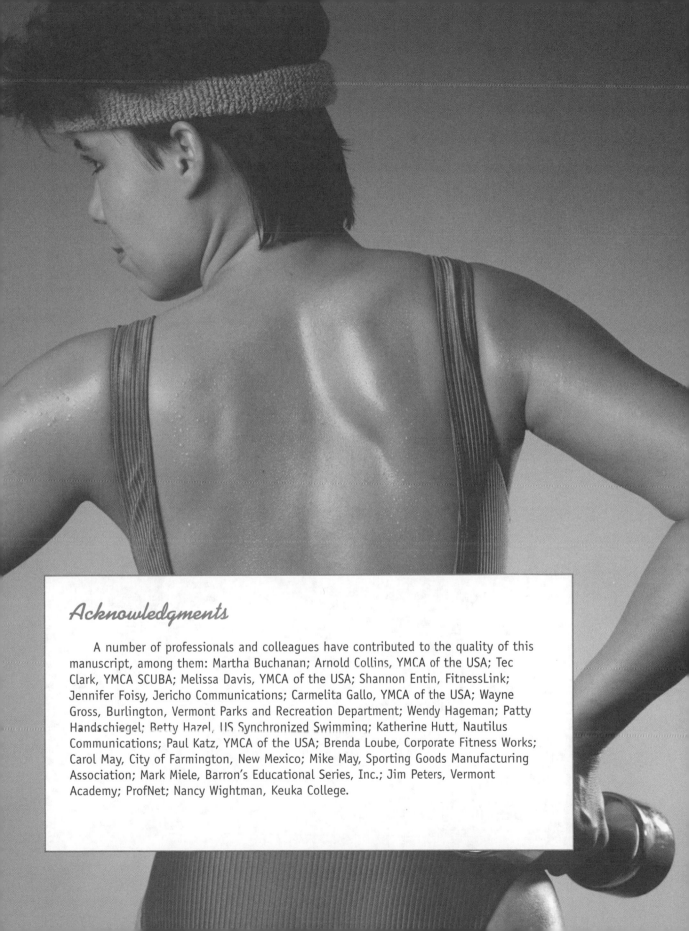

Acknowledgments

A number of professionals and colleagues have contributed to the quality of this manuscript, among them: Martha Buchanan; Arnold Collins, YMCA of the USA; Tec Clark, YMCA SCUBA; Melissa Davis, YMCA of the USA; Shannon Entin, FitnessLink; Jennifer Foisy, Jericho Communications; Carmelita Gallo, YMCA of the USA; Wayne Gross, Burlington, Vermont Parks and Recreation Department; Wendy Hageman; Patty Handschiegel; Betty Hazel, US Synchronized Swimming; Katherine Hutt, Nautilus Communications; Paul Katz, YMCA of the USA; Brenda Loube, Corporate Fitness Works; Carol May, City of Farmington, New Mexico; Mike May, Sporting Goods Manufacturing Association; Mark Miele, Barron's Educational Series, Inc.; Jim Peters, Vermont Academy; ProfNet; Nancy Wightman, Keuka College.

CHAPTER ONE

Join the Fitness Revolution

There's an uprising underway. It's not an exaggeration to call it a fight for life.

Second to smoking, weight-related conditions are the largest cause of death in the United States—some 300,000 a year. In 1980, 25 percent of all adults were overweight. Twenty years later this figure has ballooned to 34 percent, which translates to 58 million Americans with weight problems. Unhealthy weight also is considered the villain in the increase of such conditions as coronary heart disease, hypertension, gallstones, osteoarthritis, breast cancer, and colon cancer.

Medical researchers have put the cost of obesity at more than $100 billion annually, what with hospital and physician care, and the number of workdays lost to weight-related illnesses. Increasing the width of Seattle passenger ferry seats from 18 inches to 21 inches in 1999, which in turn reduced each ship's capacity from 250 passengers to 240, was an unexpected expense the Washington State ferries had to absorb.

And to this point we've covered only adults. Even more children—42 percent as opposed to 34 percent of adults—are now classified as having weight problems. What makes this statistic particularly alarming is that excess weight in children is directly related to cardiovascular disease, affecting the heart and blood vessels.

According to research developed by Shape Up America, one of a number of organizations dedicated to changing American eating and exercise habits, one out of every five teenagers is now considered "significantly overweight."

A QUICK FIX?

So desperate are many people to find a solution for their weight-related health problems that an entire industry has developed in the last several years promising rapid relief. Consumer complaints about misleading diet advertisements more than tripled between 1997 and 1999.

Not that such products are new to the market. As long ago as the 1930s cases were being brought by the Federal Trade Commission against weight loss companies promising to dissolve fat with the bath salts and massage creams they manufactured. Of course, these products did not perform as promised. But hope runs high when desperation sets in. Advertisers promising instant gratification often find ready buyers in those too impatient to spend the time a legitimate weight loss program would require to work.

Among seven companies sued in a single day by the FTC were the makers of a "Fat-Be-Gone Ring," which uses acupressure principles "equal in effect to jogging six miles"; "Slimming Insoles," which claims to press nerves in the foot that help you lose weight; and "SeQuester," which "blocks the absorption of fat by the body." Buyer beware.

But other organizations are fighting back. Shape Up America, founded in 1994 by former U.S. Surgeon General C. Everett Koop, has mushroomed to a coalition of several dozen nonprofit organizations representing such diverse interests as physical fitness, nutrition, healthcare, gardening, and the elderly, all spreading the word and creating programs to emphasize the importance of achieving a healthy weight and increasing activity levels.

HERE COME THE JOBS

You've just read some stark and dismaying statistics, but the upside is that more and more people are beginning to do something about losing weight and becoming fit.* The message these organizations want us all to hear is catching on all over the country. Even though we have a long way to go, there's a new awareness that good health, triggered by sensible eating and regular exercise, can decrease the incidence of a whole range of weight-related diseases and lengthen lives in the bargain. As a result, attendance is up at health clubs, corporate fitness centers, public and private golf clubs, city parks and swimming pools, YM(and W)CAs, and bike rental shops. The purchase of canoes and kayaks is on the rise, as well as tennis and racquetball equipment, and exercise machines. Even cruise ships, which once attracted only vacationers looking for six square meals a day and an afternoon nap in a comfortable deck chair, now have gyms and fitness programs a medium-sized city would envy; ditto large corporations and retirement homes.

*The extent to which psychological problems hinder lasting weight loss is a separate issue, and is best addressed elsewhere by those qualified to successfully deal with it.

HIGHLY RANKED ACTIVITIES

The Sporting Goods Manufacturers Association keeps close track of how many Americans participate in which sports and fitness activities, something that is obviously in its best interests. According to its most recent available figures (1999, and rounded off), the top ten most popular activities representing a significant level of potential employment for readers of this book are

1. Recreational swimming, snorkeling, SCUBA diving, etc.   108 million
2. Equipment exercise (treadmill, stationary cycling and rowing, etc.)   75 million
3. Recreational bicycling   56 million
4. Fishing (both salt- and freshwater)   54 million
5. Camping (both tent and recreational vehicle)   51 million
6. Golf   28 million
7. Kayaking, canoeing, rafting   22 million

8.	Skiing, snowboarding	22 million
9.	Soccer	18 million
10.	Tennis	17 million

Other highly ranked activities, but offering considerably fewer employment opportunities, included walking, hiking, jogging, calisthenics, inline skating, recreational basketball, bowling, volleyball, softball, and billiards.

What does all of this have to do with you? Well, somebody is going to have to train, teach, coach, manage, guide, motivate, support, and massage the muscles of the people who have decided to pursue one or more of these activities. Somebody is going to have to sell, ship, rent, stock, and maintain the equipment used. Do you see where this is going?

True, many sports, fitness, and recreation jobs—in sports medicine, for example—require education beyond a high school diploma. But many others, listed in the Table of Contents, can be accessed with a high school education.

THE IDEAL JOB

Careers in sports, recreation, and fitness represent a unique opportunity for young people not attracted to the worlds of finance and engineering, healthcare and law, marketing or human resources, or whose love of sports is not matched by a skill level that might lead to a life as a professional athlete. A definition of the "ideal job" we like is one in which you can make money doing what you'd gladly do for nothing, if you could afford to. "A man is a success," Bob Dylan once said, "if he gets up in the morning and goes to bed at night, and in between he does what he wants to."

On the following pages we've tried to pinpoint those jobs in the fields of sports, fitness, and recreation that are likely to have the most appeal to the largest number of young job seekers. If job opportunities in your sphere of interest have not been covered to your satisfaction and you have been unsuccessful in your own research efforts, contact us through the web site or e-mail address contained in the Overview of this book, and we'll steer you to a source.

We've kept in mind that most of you reading this book have decided, for one reason or another, not to attend college right now. This doesn't mean that you'll never go to college, but keep in mind that it also doesn't necessarily mean that you'll be able to get to the top of your chosen profession without additional education or training. Where the career path requires smarts difficult to acquire on the job, we'll tell you what more you need to do to get where you want to be.

You might want to check out an e-magazine called *High School* (*www.powerstudents.com*) that includes articles on job and money issues ("Beyond Burger Flipping—Finding Meaningful Employment"; "Can I Work? The Nuts and Bolts of Working as a Teen"). It also features a Sports and Fitness department.

PREPARING YOURSELF ACADEMICALLY

Plan to speak with a career or guidance counselor as soon as your interest in a specific occupation begins to crystallize, or even if you're just beginning to think about life after high school. A variety of source materials will be available to you, perhaps one or more kinds of career assessment as well. If you happen to be in a school that does not offer career assistance for whatever reason, identify the nearest public library that maintains a "career corner," or its equivalent, and introduce yourself to the librarian in charge. You may get your first exposure to computers if you haven't previously worked with them, and learn how to access career information on-line.

Brenda Loube, president of Corporate Fitness Works, Inc., which designs and manages wellness and fitness centers in six states, believes that physical education teachers also can play a role in pointing sports- and fitness-oriented students in the appropriate career direction. "Somehow," says Loube, "high school juniors and seniors need to be made aware of the business of health promotion, whether it is in the workplace, retirement facilities, or hotels, and I believe PE teachers *as well as* guidance counselors are in a unique position to spread the word." (Through Corporate Fitness Works, readers of *Success Without College: Careers in Sports, Fitness, and Recreation* have an opportunity to access mentors and internship possibilities (see page 158).

The occupations in sports and fitness vary so widely that the courses you take in preparation will depend a lot on your area of specialty. Any jobs that put you in direct contact with "customer," "member," or "client" are likely to require some knowledge of the human anatomy; therefore, such courses as biology, physiology, or anatomy will be essential. If you want to specialize in the sales or business side of these fields, however, product knowledge will be most important, as well as a rudimentary grounding in math and business principles. A golf course groundskeeper, for example, will need to know about landscape technology, pest control, and irrigation techniques, so if this is what you want to do, chemistry, biology, and physics would be helpful for you to know. As soon as you've identified a specialty, consult your guidance counselor, physical fitness instructor, or librarian for assistance in finding out more about it.

Narrowing Your Choices

It isn't enough to go to the Table of Contents, pick a sport you'd like to work in, and start looking for a job. It's going to take preparation, and plenty of it. Still, if you plan ahead and know what to look for, your assignment becomes more manageable.

PERSONALITY TESTS

First of all, what kind of job matches your personality? Your high school guidance counselor can help here, or you can find out something about yourself on your own if you have access to a computer.

1. After getting on-line, type *http://www.keirsey.com* in the address line.

2. Scroll down to "The Keirsey Temperament Sorter II," ten lines from the top, and click again. The questionnaire that appears consists of 70 questions, which should be answered as honestly as possible. Your answers will be matched against the four personality types, or "temperaments," listed on the second page of the Keirsey site.

3. Take your four-letter temperament indicator to: *www.doi.gov/octc/typescar.html* to see a list of possible vocations that match your letter grouping.

Remember that the Keirsey questionnaire measures *preferences*, not *skills*, meaning that there are no right or wrong answers. You may use them on your own, or share them with whomever you choose. Similarly, because the questionnaire deals with preferences, no one personality type is better than another. Each has the potential to lead you to a rich and successful career, in a way that lines you up with the kinds of work you are apt to prefer. Also, your responses are confidential. So use the results of your explorations as a general guide. They will provide clues to get you started in the right direction, but shouldn't be considered the *only* way to go. Some people have many interests, for example, and are not successfully categorized with a single four-letter profile.

You're not going to see many specific sport- or fitness-related job titles on any of the lists under the 16 respective personality types, but you will learn about some of the types of work likely to suit you. If your personality type is "ESFJ" (The "E" stands for "extrovert"; you'll learn what the other letters stand for after you take the test), athletic coach and massage therapist are two of the listed careers—but these are exceptions. Instead you'll see more general occupations under the various personality types, which can then be applied to several of the careers treated in this book. For example, six of the sixteen types include such vocation areas as administrator, office manager, sales manager, franchise owner, promoter, and sales trainer. All of these easily fall under the grouping of the retail-oriented job titles, bicycle, kayak, and golf shop sales, rental, and repair, among others.

By the way, the U.S. Office of the Interior sponsors a complete job search strategy site called Career Manager, of which the Kiersey Personality Instrument is just a part. (The home page is at *www.doi.gov/octc/index.html*.) You can learn more about the basic job-hunting tools of networking, job fairs, résumés and cover letters, interview tips, and relocation, many of which are covered as well in Chapters Seven, Eight, and Nine of *Success Without College: Careers in Sports, Fitness, and Recreation*.

SHADOWING AN EXPERT

Many schools invite professionals from the community to share their working environment for a day or more with interested students. This is a considerably more meaningful version of the Career Day presentations some of you may remember from elementary school days, where your dad or mom appeared on cue to describe a day in his or her working life, sometimes in painful detail, at least from your perspective. Today's "shadow programs"— either as a career guidance effort, or sponsored by various parent-teacher organizations—are much more practical, and permit students to experience firsthand a general idea of what goes on in the daily life of an individual who holds a job of special interest to them. If such programs are not available in your school, talk to your homeroom teacher or a guidance counselor about getting one established.

INFORMATION INTERVIEWS

If you are unable to investigate the career that interests you through a shadow program, ask family members or friends to give you the names of three or more people who hold jobs in the career that interests you, or better yet, who started there but have since moved on to positions of greater responsibility and challenge. Ask such potential source people if they would be willing to speak with you for a half hour or more about what they do, preferably in their place of work. This is what professionals at all levels do, by the way, when they have decided to change careers but have not yet determined exactly what specific direction is right for them. This meeting is called an *information interview*, and is a great way to get firsthand intelligence from the people on the firing line. Here's how to make it happen:

Let's say you've been thinking about a career in massage therapy. You see from Chapter Six of this book that many massage therapists start as assistants, right out of high school. You've discussed this with your family, and one evening at dinner your dad mentions that a friend at work has a daughter, now working as a licensed massage therapist, who got a job just out of high school as a massage therapist assistant.

"My friend said Ellen would be happy to talk with you about it," says your dad. "Just give her a call."

Now you need to prepare thoroughly for your information interview, to get as much out of it as possible, and at the same time not waste the time of the professional who was gracious enough to see you. First decide what it is about being a massage therapist (substitute your own occupational preference) that would help you decide whether or not to get into the profession. Some possible questions:

- How did you happen to get into massage therapy?

- When did you first know you wanted to be a massage therapist?

- What pitfalls did you have to deal with along the way? (Financial problems? Finding enough time to change careers while you were in another job?)

- What do you like most about being a massage therapist?

- What was the most difficult part about going from massage therapy assistant to massage therapist?

- What is your typical workday like (if there is such a thing)?

- What are your personal career goals?

- Are there any other career paths open to a massage therapy assistant? What are they?

- Can you think of any good books or videos on massage therapy that would help me?

- Do you have any other suggestions to help me decide whether to get into this field?

Stick to important issues, and try to avoid time-wasting questions such as "How much vacation do you get?" or "Do you have to pay for your own uniforms?" (Read that section of the chapter that deals with your specialty before preparing questions.) If you find your source to be informative and cooperative, ask if it would be all right for you to call him or her when you graduate, for possible job-search recommendations or information on job openings. Don't forget to ask each interviewee for a business card to more easily make contact for follow-up information. Also, ask if there are two or three other individuals in the same occupation who might also be willing to talk with you. Finally, be sure to write a thank you letter to your source person for taking the time to answer your questions and giving you such good advice.

VOLUNTEERING

It may be that one of your information interviews leads to someone in a position to let you work in the occupation that interests you. It may also be that the employer does not have an opening for an assistant, but would be willing to let you hang out on a regular basis, just to see what the job is all about.

If you are a sophomore, junior, or senior, this can be an experience crucial to your future professional life. Not only do you get a feel for the ups and downs of the job, but if it turns out you like it enough to find a real job in that field when you graduate, this volunteering experience looks very good on your résumé (see Chapter Seven), and could just make the difference in the boss's decision whether to hire you or the candidate he saw yesterday. And if you didn't like the experience well enough to continue in the field, start at the beginning and try again with an occupation better suited to your interests or skills.

INTERNSHIPS

Thanks to the federal government's Schools-To-Careers program, schools in more and more states are developing formal internship programs to ease a transition to the workplace for students who don't intend to go immediately to a community or four-year college directly after graduation. If your school has not yet put a program together, a number of other schools with programs in place have put them on the Internet for others to share. Salem High School, in Salem, New Hampshire, is one. It has prepared internship worksheets in six areas, "Schools-To-Careers" being the program of most interest to you at this time. All of the goals of internship are there, along with "responsibilities," which is more a checklist of things to remember to make sure the internship program is as effective as possible, that the writers have charted for students, parents, business, school mentors, and the high school administration. You can access other schools' internships with your favorite search engine if you, your guidance counselor, or physical education teacher would like to examine other points of view.

WHAT'S CONTAINED IN THIS BOOK

Following this chapter is a list of the sport, fitness, and recreation occupations that may interest you, as well as the various kinds of employers in those occupations. Some are covered in detail in this book. For those lower on the popularity list we've provided source material that will enable you to investigate further on your own.

We've organized the book this way to give you some idea of the wide variety of working conditions possible in your specialty. These occupations fall under a number of different categories, listed in Chapters Two through Six. There is some inevitable overlap among them, in that most of these jobs exist not only under the setting described in that chapter, but sometimes under two or three other categories as well. For example, we included the YMCA SCUBA program in Chapter Three, Careers in Public Service Organizations, rather than in Chapter Four, Careers In, On, and Near the Water, because it is a world-renowned SCUBA program closely associated with the Y.

In each of the specialty chapters, Two through Six, you'll meet several professionals in the field who got their start at an entry level before moving on to positions of greater responsibility. You'll find out why they do what they do, what got them where they are, and what parts of their jobs they like—and don't like.

The companies or organizations included in each specialty chapter were selected to give the flavor of the jobs and the circumstances under which they are performed. Together with the profiles of the men and women whose professional lives are described in each chapter, this offers the best opportunity to let you know what a job is "really" like.

Each of the people profiled has faced a career dilemma of some kind, at least once, and in some cases, several times. Through their stories you'll see ways to get closer to your professional goal, if you have identified one yet, none by itself necessarily the only way. More important, you'll learn that a false start or two at the beginning of your working life need not stifle your dreams for the sports, fitness, or recreation career you are now seeking.

So, in the next five specialty chapters we'll give you a taste of some of the sports, fitness, and recreation jobs out there; in the last three chapters we'll show you how to most effectively go after those that interest you most. Before you get started, just for fun log on to *www.sportsworld.com*, where more than 100 U.S. and Canadian jobs will be listed at any one time, all of which remain posted for 90 days. You'll get a better idea of what exists in your specialty at any given time.

A FEW KEY POINTS TO REMEMBER

• Make preliminary career choice decisions by comparing the work to be done with your own personality and interests.

• When in doubt, take career tests to help you determine what kinds of jobs you would be good at.

• As soon as your interest in a particular occupation begins to develop, talk to your high school guidance counselor or physical education teacher about the variety of source materials available to you.

• Investigate "shadow" programs and volunteer opportunities, and conduct information interviews to find out about specific occupations.

WHERE THE JOBS ARE

Settings

Occupations	Bicycle/Ski Shop	City/County Park Department	Corporate Fitness Center	Cruise Ship	Fishing Lodge	Golf Club	Grade School/High School	Hospital Fitness Center	Hotel Fitness Center	Public Service Organization	Private Fitness Center	Ski Resort	Swimming Club	Whitewater Outfitter
Aerobics Instructor			•	•				•		•				
Aquatics Director		•		•						•		•		
Bicycle Mechanic	•													
Bike Shop Sales and Repair	•													
Camp Director		•								•				
Canoe/Kayak Instructor		•			•					•			•	
Exercise Room Supervisor			•	•				•		•				
Fishing Guide					•								•	
Fitness Instructor			•	•				•		•				
Greenskeeper		•				•								
Hunting Guide													•	
Lifeguard		•		•						•		•		
Martial Arts Instructor			•	•						•	•			
Massage Therapist			•	•				•			•	•		
Personal Trainer			•	•				•		•				
Pool Supervisor		•		•						•		•		
Rock Climbing Instructor		•								•	•		•	
Ropes Course Instructor		•								•	•		•	
Recreational Guide		•								•			•	
River Guide		•			•								•	
SCUBA Instructor				•						•		•		
Ski/Snowboard Sales and Repair	•										•			
Soccer Official		•					•	•						•
Sports Public Relations						•				•	•			
Synchronized Swimming Instructor							•						•	•
Whitewater Guide					•								•	

CHAPTER TWO

Private Fitness Centers

The growing number of private health clubs and fitness centers over the past several years has largely to do with the fitness revolution described in Chapter One. Today these facilities are located not only downtown and in neighborhood malls, but in retirement homes, corporate headquarters, hotels, resorts, and on cruise ships. If people are motivated to work out and don't have home gyms, there are alternatives, no matter where a person happens to be.

There are other reasons these fitness centers are sprouting up around the country. First of all, there is money to be made, and plenty of it. According to Medical Fitness Association figures, nearly 30 percent of all hospital fitness centers are set up on a for-profit basis. "We have identified a total market of 13 million adults with the need and the financial wherewithal to be involved in such centers," says John P. Greene, MFA's executive director. "With millions of baby boomers entering retirement age, we see medical fitness having the potential to create a revenue stream of $7.3 billion a year."

This means jobs, lots of jobs. So if your occupation interest shows up in some of the categories in the chart on page 13 as you read the rest of this chapter, put it on your list of target employers when you get to Chapter Eight, Marketing Yourself into a Good Job.

COMMERCIAL FITNESS CENTERS

The Santa Cruz, California, business directory lists 28 "physical fitness facilities." They include gyms, yoga centers, dance studios, and health spas. For a city of 55,717, this averages out to one facility for nearly 2,000 citizens. New Haven, Connecticut, names five such facilities for twice as many people, or one for every 24,600 citizens, although more than a dozen others are available in the immediate suburbs. What does this mean? If you're interested in finding a job in a private health club, your chances of success may depend a lot on where you live; it may also mean that research probably will be one of your most important job-search tools.

Physical fitness facilities feature exercise and weight loss programs, gyms, health clubs, and day spas. These establishments also frequently offer aerobic dance, yoga, and exercise classes. The facilities may be open to the public or offered on a membership basis. Sports and recreation clubs open only to members and their guests include some golf, yacht, tennis, racquetball, hunt clubs, and gun clubs. Public golf courses, unlike private clubs, offer facilities to the general public on a fee basis.

A Person Who's Done It

MEET CHARLIE LARSON

VITAL STATISTICS

After he got out of high school, Charlie Larson went through a string of unsatisfying jobs. He worked in the North Dakota oil fields, in a machine shop on the Texas-Mexico border, in a San Francisco rock band, and in various other locations as a security guard, bicycle messenger, and in a tea packaging warehouse, finally ending up in a large machine shop and metals factory in northern Illinois. Years later, on a bench press in a Los Angeles gym, it finally occurred to Charlie what he wanted to do. Today, with most of his professional story yet to be written, Charlie's decision has brought him to a very different place in his life.

It's difficult to explain why I left [the Illinois factory]. I was running a million dollar robotics line in the machine shop, and had quite a bit of responsibility. At that point there was a lot of fear among the machinists that robotics was going to eliminate jobs. When you think about it, you realize that more often, the opposite is the case: Increased efficiency makes the company more competitive, creates more revenue, and allows management to consider additional product lines, which in turn *increases* the number of jobs.

So apparently, word got upstairs, and the president asked me to act as one of the liaisons between management and the machinists. I spoke to groups of employees from the point of view of the machinists on individual projects. The speeches went over really well, and before long I was speaking at corporate factories in Chicago and Minnesota.

This was exhilarating, and I was good at it—just being able to talk to people, and see their interest peak. But eventually I was sent back to my "real job" on the robotics line, and that was a major letdown. After a vacation in Mexico, I decided to quit. I just couldn't stand going back to that grind, even though I liked the people.

The thing I learned from that experience was that it was possible to have fun and make a living at the same time. I had had a taste of that, and it was taken away from me.

I spent the next few months depressed that I would never be able to find a full-time job that I loved and would be paid to do. My sister in Los Angeles said, "Come out here, Charlie. My home is small, but my heart is big."

That's what I did, and when I got there all I did for the first couple of weeks was rollerblade, lift weights, and read. I had been lifting weights since I was 20, and I love the gym environment. And all the while I was lifting or rollerblading, I was waiting for this flash to hit me and let me know what this perfect job would be. In the gym one day I was on the bench press, thinking that nobody was going to pay me to lift weights, and it actually happened. I looked over and saw a personal trainer giving a client some instruction, and thought: "Wow. This is it! I can be in the gym, which I like a lot; and I can help other people, which I also like a lot." I decided to go for it.

The first course I took was at the L.A. Athletic Club, with an organization called Progressive Fitness. It was a 40-hour, American Council on Exercise (ACE) accredited program. My instructor was Sam Calhoun, who had the title "America's Most Muscular Man" in 1959. He's been in the fitness industry for more than 35 years, and his certifications go into double digits. He was my basic teacher—and he's the greatest, one of those guys who inspires, an extremely knowledgeable man, and a great mentor.

This course was a comprehensive review of theory, personal training, and practical training. It's a preparation course for the certification program, but I underestimated the amount of basic knowledge that was required, and didn't pass the test. OK, I thought, I'm going to do this right, so I took a 60-hour personal training internship in Long Beach, at Gold's Gym, also under Sam Calhoun, and felt really confident when I went back to take the test. This time I passed it. The course cost $1,200, but it was worth it. Since then I've studied nutrition too, and I just took six courses at the IDEA Personal Trainer Summit West 2000.

Unfortunately, there are a lot of unqualified people in personal training. And there's a lot to keep in mind. You have to have insurance; you have to have a valid certification.

I see trainers teaching unsound principles. A lot of them get their "certification" from a weekend course, and then after taking a watered-down test, they're certified—just enough to cover them legally. You have to have a really good understanding of kinesiology (the study of anatomy and body movement, especially as it relates to physical education or therapy).

One thing I knew before I went into this was that I wanted a strong knowledge base before I trained my first client. I wanted to really understand. And it's not just to cover myself in case of a lawsuit; it's because I really care. I don't want somebody to get hurt under my direction. To me, that means more than anything. I think that should be every personal trainer's top priority. They say the four criteria for good training are:

1. It needs to be safe.
2. It needs to be habit-forming.
3. It needs to get results.
4. It needs to be time-conscious (within the client's time schedule).

My first job was at a franchise of a major fitness chain. It provides insurance coverage for its trainers and its facilities are incredible, with some very sophisticated equipment. If you can afford to go in the off-hours, I couldn't recommend a better club. And the club provides insurance coverage for its trainers, which is great. The club sells a lot of memberships, and the membership price is reasonable. When you're there as a member during prime hours in the evening, though, roughly from 4:00 to 9:00 P.M. on Mondays, Tuesdays, and Wednesdays, it can get crowded, which from the point of view of the trainer, leaves very little time for individual client attention. This may be one of the reasons this company is somewhat of a stepping-stone for some trainers.

When I was at the club and finished with each of my clients, I'd ask, "Do you think you got your money's worth?" And they'd say, "Totally," or something similar. That was a great feeling. Also, after I had been working with a client for a while, always explaining in detail the advice I was giving, I'd spot someone doing a lift or exercise incorrectly, and ask my client, "What do you see about that person's form that is lacking?" or "What is she doing that is potentially dangerous?" It was fun to hear the client say something like, "That could cause a shoulder injury over time." Those were times I knew I was doing good teaching.

Anyway, now I'm ready for my breakthrough. It could be on my own, or with another club. The marketing part of going into business for myself is something I'm still learning. But I'll get there. The motivation was already in place. Now I have the knowledge base and the experience, too.

HOSPITAL FITNESS CENTERS

The top three reasons mature people select a hospital-affiliated fitness center, says a survey by Chicago's Galter Life Center, are

- to improve their fitness level

- to reduce their health risk

- to increase their energy level

Hospital fitness centers provide rehabilitation services for stroke victims, or those who have had joint replacement or other surgeries. They also offer preventive and therapeutic rehabilitation for conditions such as heart disease, diabetes, arthritis, obesity, and hypertension. It is as a preventive outlet that they are able to compete successfully with traditional privately owned fitness centers. Allied health professionals usually are available for consultation and testing. The in-center snack bars often feature snacks and drinks with an eye toward dietary needs and considerations.

Some hospital fitness centers surpass commercial centers in size and services offered. The recently completed 69,000-square-foot rehab/wellness facility at Community Hospital in Munster, Indiana, features a five-lane lap pool, multipurpose gym, climbing wall, and children's play area. The Delnor-Community Health and Wellness Center in Geneva, Illinois, asks every new member to complete a health assessment before using any of the facilities. The test evaluates fat-to-lean ratio, cardiovascular conditioning, endurance, flexibility, and cholesterol levels. An exercise physiologist then creates an individualized activity program based on the computerized report, with periodic evaluations. Membership fees and services are not inexpensive: At Delnor-Community, the initial health assessment costs $250 for an individual, $375 for a couple or family. Monthly dues for an individual are $68 for an individual, $106 for a couple, and $137 for a family.

CORPORATE FITNESS CENTERS

Let's say *you* are doing the hiring. Want to impress your top job candidates? Make the corporate fitness center a highlight of the company tour. This is what more and more organizations are doing to lure good people away from competing companies. The fitness center has become one of the leading benefits many candidates use to differentiate between two otherwise equally attractive employers.

From the company point of view, the regular, company-sponsored physical activity available in the corporate fitness center can pay financial dividends. The primary value of such activity, of course, is that it improves employee performance and morale, and at the same time reduces employee downtime due to sick days. This is both tangible and significant, as has been documented by numerous studies.

Since the early 1980s Richmond, Virginia, GE Financial Assurance has maintained an on-site fitness center for its employees. In that time, the employee population has almost doubled, from 600 to 1,100. GEFA wanted to do two things: (1) maintain its strategic advantage in attracting top talent; and (2) continue to offer an effective and creative physical fitness program for all of its employees. The answer was a state-of-the-art, 6,200-square-foot facility that was completed in 1998.

Companies also have found that fitness centers can significantly help cut insurance claims, workplace injuries, and workers' compensation claims. After a two-year study, Coca-Cola Company found that claims filed by employees who were regulars at HealthWorks, its corporate headquarters fitness center in Atlanta, averaged $535 per year less than those who were either occasional members or nonmembers.

HOTEL FITNESS CENTERS

Management for the larger hotels are learning that spiffy fitness centers mean increased business. Most large hotels have installed them, and those that haven't are either building them or losing customers. In the major metropolitan areas, chambers of commerce and other municipal groups interested in their community's economic welfare make sure the word gets out. The Yellow Page listing for most hotels with fitness centers will usually include it, as will the hotel's web site. Some city web sites include a listing of all hotels with fitness centers. In New Orleans, for example, the web site page listing all "hotels with great fitness facilities" is *www.aroomforyou.com/fitness.htm*; in Chicago, the site is "Chicago Hotels with Top Fitness Centers," or *www.stayinchicago.com/fitness.htm*. Both of these sites, and probably the one in your metropolitan area as well, rate the facilities and specify the available services.

A Person
Who's Done It

MEET NANCY KENNEDY

VITAL STATISTICS

As an extremely underweight youngster, Nancy Kennedy suffered from low self-esteem. Not until her first trip to the gym did she see a way to lose the self-consciousness that had been part of her life since she was a little girl. Before she realized her dream job she waited tables, worked in retail, kept books, and answered phones. Finally she reached her goal: personal trainer. Ultimately, she worked her way up to become president of her own successful fitness and nutrition company, and was recently named "Best Personal Trainer in L.A." by Los Angeles *magazine, with a fitness center in the Sofitel Hotel. It happened this way:*

I was very thin as a young girl, which most people don't want to hear for some reason. It had made me incredibly uncomfortable, even though I had been a model since the age of seven. And I remained uncomfortable until my then-husband talked me into going to the gym. I fell in love with it immediately, both with the way I felt and the power that feeling gave me. The more I went, the more I was intrigued with feeling like nothing in the world I'd ever experienced.

I sort of "graduated" to Gold's Gym, in Venice, California, where I got the fitness bug for good, and was certified in 1992 through the Aerobics and Fitness Association of America (AFAA). I was also fortunate enough to meet a girl who owned her private training gym. She took me under her wing, and taught me a tremendous amount, including how to put a routine together and how to work with a client. I was also quick enough to realize that she took almost all of the fee that the gym charged, and that I could have been making $40 an hour instead of the $15 an hour she was paying me.

She charged me a "floor fee" plus a percentage of the hourly fee, because the clients came to her. That's a bigger bite than most gym owners take. Most training gyms typically charge a flat hourly fee to use the facility, with no additional percentage.

I stayed for six months, and left with one client, who was the best client I could have had. First of all, he was extremely overweight, and with my help he slimmed down nicely, which is the best kind of advertisement a trainer can have. Second, he knew a lot of people in the entertainment business, and told everybody how good he felt and how great I was. Well, people could easily see that he looked a lot better, and my phone started ringing off the hook. Through that client I met a costume designer, and we became good friends.

I was with her for about three months when she was assigned to do a film on location with Julia Roberts. About a week before she left, she called and said: "Julia needs a trainer. Are you interested?"

About a week later a limo drove up to my door to go to the airport, and off we went. And that pretty much started my business on a completely different direction. I trained Julia on location in Chicago first for two weeks, and then to Wisconsin for three weeks, then back to Chicago, and then back here to L.A. I took a very big chance, because I had to walk away from a number of clients to make that trip. No other trainers worked for me then; it was just me.

But it worked out fine. I learned a lot about the business, and the following year I was named one of the best fitness trainers in the country. At the next gym I went to I met Bobby Strom, who had a body-building and nutrition background that complemented my own. He became my business partner, and earlier this year we were married—so now we're partners 24/7!

Another client I was training at about that time managed the Hotel Sofitel, in West Los Angeles. One day she asked me to come over and help her, and when I got there she took me down to a storage room, and said, "I'm thinking of putting a gym in here."

The place was about 3,000 square feet. I said, "You've got to be kidding me!"

"Would you design it?" she asked.

So we installed a full range of cardiovascular equipment, including top-of-the-line treadmills, stationary bikes, recumbent bikes, and Stairmasters. We've been here three and a half years and have fourteen trainers. We see hotel guests come back over and over again because of this amazing state-of-the-art gym, which most hotels do not have. And the hotel management paid for everything!

Through another client I met Dr. David Heber, a world-renowned nutritionist now at UCLA. Dr. Heber told my client that he was impressed with the amount of body fat she was able to exchange for lean muscle. He wanted to know who she was working with. That was probably my best introduction. Dr. Heber also treats breast cancer and general cancer patients, and thanks to him I now work with a number of cancer survivors. This is the most rewarding client base that I serve. To prepare adequately I became a certified food handler, and took courses from the Los Angeles Department of Health, as well as from other recognized nutrition organizations.

About a year and a half ago a big health club called Crunch asked us to prepare a line of healthy fast foods they wanted to sell. I love to cook, and had first started preparing meals when I was on location with Julia Roberts. She and I trained together early in the morning, and from 6:00 A.M. on I had absolutely nothing to do, so I'd cook healthy meals for her to take on the set. Later I did the same thing on location with other clients, and got a lot of press about it, which is why the Crunch people got in touch with us. This enterprise has snowballed—to the point where we have an amazing commercial kitchen in downtown Los Angeles that makes all of our recipes and our labels.

I've been really fortunate throughout my career. I've learned to keep my eyes and ears open, which I think is particularly important for people without a college degree. I think I'm a really good example in that I have a high school education, like the readers of this book. And even though I've picked up two years of junior college along the way, I learned so much on my own. This was mostly because I identified a passion and then became focused about it. I can't get enough information, and I go to as many conferences and conventions as I have time for. I continue to learn every day. I think this is one of the biggest reasons I've been successful.

CRUISE SHIP FITNESS CENTERS

Everybody's dream job: to be on a floating resort all year-round, and take money for it. In 1972 teenager Mary Fallon Miller took her first cruise. She and her family crossed the Atlantic on the SS *France*, and Mary won a "Junior Reporter" competition with her story on the number of croissants baked daily. The experience began an obsession with cruise line travel that years later led to her writing *How to Sail Around the World on Luxury Cruise Ships and Get Paid for It,* now in its fifth edition.

Fallon paints a glamorous picture of shipboard life, and for many cruise company employees it is a true picture. Ship doctors, entertainers, chefs, and cruise directors are paid well. Entry-level jobs pay less well, and the turnover is large; still, for many this is an excellent way to see parts of the world that might not be accessible otherwise, as well as learn new skills that may be transferable to other industries and specialties.

There are also watchdogs for the industry, who try to keep consumers informed about the state of cruise ship travel, including inconsistencies in service. Jason Higley, for example, keeps track of cruise ship companies out of Florida. In addition to offering advice on what to wear and how much to tip, he criticizes companies when he thinks they deserve it. In one of his on-line reports, Higley says of Cape Canaveral Cruise Line: "They didn't have enough money to repair the hull of their cruise ship, which were (sic) estimated in the millions." And of Premier Cruises: "Had two ships seized by creditors overseas and stranded thousands of passengers, many of whom had to fly back to the U.S. on charter planes. All cruises are canceled. Hotel vouchers are no longer valid."

One link to this site takes viewers directly to the 260 crew members *still* stranded as a result of the ships' seizing: "The real story of the *Seawind Crown*, as experienced by us, the crew," included some disturbing descriptions of physical conditions aboard a ship long vacated by the passengers. Is this a trend, or an isolated incident? Hard to say. But it tells you to research not just a prospective employer, but the industry itself as you consider your alternatives.

FINDING WORK IN A PRIVATE FITNESS CENTER

If you are certified as a fitness or aerobics instructor, personal trainer, or martial arts instructor, you're not likely to have trouble getting work in a privately owned health club—and you can probably find work just about anywhere you want to live. Opportunities also exist, although somewhat fewer of them, for yoga instructors, pool operators, lifeguards, and massage therapists, among others. At the entry level, though, your options are reduced to jobs such as receptionist, equipment handler, assistants where they are needed, and maintenance positions. If you're a sophomore, junior, or senior in high school, you may have a shot at an internship in some of the bigger clubs. Larger aerobics and fitness classes may call for assistants, maybe just to pass out towels. If you've had a class or two, or are a "natural," though, your chances improve. If you can afford to volunteer three or four hours a week, they improve even more, and the experience looks great on your résumé.

Networking organizations and job-search web sites for specific occupations are listed by category in Chapter Eight, Marketing Yourself into a Good Job. Four fitness-related web sites worth a close look are:

- **Aerobics and Fitness Association of America** (*www.afaa.com*)
  For both fitness professionals and enthusiasts. Has certified more than 145,000 fitness professionals. Offers 2,500 workshops annually. Certifies aerobics instructors, personal trainers, step instructors, weight training instructors, and kickboxing instructors.

- **American Fitness Professionals and Associates** (*www.AFPAfitness.com*) Accredited certification agency conducting continuing education conferences and seminars. Excellent career section including job descriptions, education, and employment possibilities for a dozen fitness careers. Comparative information for top certification agencies, including cost, knowledge, and practical experience required, and testing options.

- **IDEA, Inc.** (*www.ideafit.com*) "Your source for professional fitness information." Comprehensive catalog of fitness, health, and wellness-related magazines and journals, latest trends, classifieds and employment opportunities, and answers to frequently asked questions. Conducts conferences and workshops to upgrade professional skills.

- **Pro's Center Fitness Link** (*www.fitnesslinkpros.com*) Complete job descriptions for a variety of fitness occupations. Extensive information regarding skills required, educational requirements, hours, salary, employment options, and sources for additional job-related data. Links to other fitness organizations, as well as means to professional growth through continuing education, workshops, and conventions.

A FEW KEY POINTS TO REMEMBER

- The fitness revolution has made entry-level jobs available in a wide variety of facilities, not only in private health clubs and fitness centers, but also in retirement homes, corporate headquarters, hotels, resorts, and on cruise ships.

- Entry-level jobs in these facilities usually involve positions such as receptionist, equipment handler, assistant, and maintenance person.

- While a job as a fitness or aerobic instructor, personal trainer, or martial arts instructor does not require a college education, you will need certification to attain these positions.

- What to learn from Charlie: (1) It may take a while, but you can find a permanent, full-time job that you love, and you can get paid to do it. (2) You need a strong knowledge base, motivation, and marketing skills to be successful in the fitness field.

- What to learn from Nancy: (1) Keep your eyes and ears open. You can learn so much on your own by watching other successful people. (2) Focus on your passion and get as much information as you can; go to conferences and conventions, and take the courses you need.

CHAPTER THREE

Careers in Public Service Organizations

There are many job opportunities in the dozens of not-for-profit organizations created to help others, or to advance a cause, or both. Often the wages aren't as good as the for-profit companies pay, but the work can be extremely rewarding, and at this stage of your professional life, it is an excellent opportunity to spend time with people whose primary motivation is to improve other people's lives. The following organizations all can be accessed on the Internet at the addresses indicated. Most will answer your career-related questions; some also include a "job opportunities" page, or something similar.

PUBLIC SERVICE GROUPS WITH JOBS

- **American Alliance for Health, Physical Education, Recreation, and Dance.** Represents six national associations and six district associations, supporting and assisting the achievement of a healthy lifestyle for those involved in physical education, leisure, fitness, dance, health promotion, and education (*www.aahperd.org*).

• **Black Women in Sport Foundation.** Encourages young black women to realize their potential in whatever sport interests them, and uses their sports participation and successes as a way to raise self-esteem and foster success in other life endeavors (*www.mcsgnet.com/bwsf/home.htm*).

• **Boys and Girls Clubs of America.** Helps youth of all backgrounds, with special concern for those from disadvantaged circumstances, develop the qualities needed to become responsible citizens and leaders (*www.bgca.org*).

• **Camp Fire Boys and Girls.** Builds on the strength of their councils to positively impact the development of children and youth through community-based youth development programs (*www.campfire.org/campfire_ns4.html*).

• **National Association for Girls and Women in Sport** (See *www.aahperd.org*).

• **Special Olympics International.** Provides year-round sports training and athletic competition in a variety of Olympic-type sports for individuals with mental retardation by giving them continuing opportunities to develop physical fitness, demonstrate courage, experience joy, and participate in a sharing of gifts, skills, and friendship with their families, other Special Olympics athletes, and the community (*www.specialolympics.org*).

• **Women's Sports Foundation.** Addresses the needs of professional and amateur women in sports, including expanding opportunities for girls and women, gender discrimination, girls playing on boys' teams, and sports media coverage (*www.womenssportsfoundation.org*).

- **YMCA of the USA.** As the largest not-for-profit community service organization in the country, works to meet the health and social service needs of 17.5 million men, women, and children members (*www.ymca.net*).

- **YWCA of the USA.** Committed to empower women and girls and to eliminate racism. Provides opportunities for girls to develop their social, athletic, and leadership skills through such grassroots programs as basketball, volleyball, tennis, soccer, softball, field hockey, aquatics, and artistic and rhythmic gymnastics. Other programs include a healthy lifestyles education program, human sexuality/pregnancy prevention sessions, first aid classes, and other physical and mental health services (*www.ywca.org*).

(See Appendix A on pages 157–159 for a complete list of sports- and fitness-related organizations.)

YMCA

Quick . . . who invented the game of basketball?

You may have remembered that James Naismith originated the game of basketball, using peach baskets nailed to pieces of wood as targets for players' shots. But did you also know that Naismith was an instructor at the YMCA Training School when he wrote the first set of basketball rules in 1891? Today that school is Springfield College, in Massachusetts.

The director at the time asked Naismith to come up with a winter game to occupy a class of incorrigible teenagers. These were kids used to rugby and football, certainly not interested in leapfrog or tumbling, the traditional inside winter games of the time. Naismith decided that the new game had to be physically active and simple to understand. It could not be rough (because of the nature of the group for whom the game was being devised), so no contact was allowed. The ball could be passed but not carried. Goals at each end of the court would involve skill and science. Elevating the goal would eliminate rushes that could injure players, a problem in both rugby and football. Naismith introduced the game of basketball at the next gym class.

The boys loved it, and introduced the game to their hometown friends over Christmas break. Naismith's invention spread like wildfire, and is one of the most popular games played—and watched—today. Volleyball and racquetball are Y inventions as well. Volleyball first came into being a few miles up the road from Springfield in Holyoke, Massachusetts. Racquetball was invented in the Greenwich, Connecticut, Y, by a member who couldn't find squash players at his level and didn't like handball.

YMCAs are an important part of community life in towns and cities all across the country. They teach kids to swim, offer exercise classes for both the able-bodied and people with disabilities, and lead adult aerobics. They also offer hundreds of other programs that vary with the needs of the communities being served, among them camping and child care. Nearly 2,400 Ys are run by 61,000 volunteer policymakers serving on boards and committees, plus more than a half million other volunteer program leaders—all working with paid professional staff members. The Y's national operating budget in 1999 was $3.5 billion.

Here are the major Y programs available in most, but not all, communities:

- **Aquatics.** Swimming lessons, SCUBA instruction (see pages 40–46), competitive swimming

- **Arts and Humanities.** Writing, performing, visual arts

- **Camping.** Day, overnight, nature hikes, computer classes (see pages 35–38)

- **Child Care.** Infant, toddler, preschool, school-age, and combinations

- **Community Development.** Job training, drug abuse prevention, development programs

- **Family.** Family nights, support groups and programs

- **Health and Fitness.** Group exercise, strength training, martial arts, yoga, personal fitness

- **International.** Educational exchanges and programs, international fairs

- **Older Adults.** Health and fitness, social clubs, volunteering

- **Sports.** Youth and adults: basketball, soccer, baseball/T-ball

- **Teen Leadership.** Clubs, adventure programs, Black achievers, Earth Service Corps, Leader Clubs, Hi-Y, Youth and Government, Model United Nations, middle school programs

CAMPING PROGRAMS

YMCAs became involved in camping in the 1860s, when a youth director took a group of boys to Lake Champlain, in Vermont. The oldest Y camp is Camp Dudley, established in 1886 on the New York side of Lake Champlain. Today, 115 summers or so later, YMCA day and overnight camps are still using the experience to make new friends, build new skills, and grow in self-reliance. Many Y camps use the natural environment to teach youth about the wonders of the world around them and how they can take good care of it. Some offer special sessions on academics, sports, arts, or teen adventure or leadership.

One camp with more than 75 years of history, at Sherman Lake, Michigan, began in 1925 as a Boy Scout camp. When the Boy Scouts moved to nearby Kalamazoo in the 1980s, a group of volunteers collaborated to create a youth camp center, later to become the Sherman Lake YMCA Outdoor Center.

Today, this 300-acre facility, on the wooded shores of Lake Sherman, supports a number of programs for both day campers and overnighters. Among the activities regularly enjoyed are canoeing, kayaking, soccer, basketball, volleyball, archery, nature appreciation, hiking, sailing, rollerblading, fishing, swimming, tennis, horseback riding, fitness, and leadership development, among others. A six-lane indoor pool with two diving boards complements water sports on the lake. In the same building is a gymnasium with an indoor climbing wall, fitness rooms, and a basketball court. The Mawby Equestrian Center houses 12 horses for summer riding. There's not much in the way of camp-oriented activity that young people and adults aren't able to enjoy at Sherman Lake. For a more complete look at the Sherman Lake YMCA Outdoor Center and its programs, view their web site at: *www.shermanlakeymca.org.*

"What sets us apart at Sherman Lake," says director of camp services Bob Campbell, "is our educational program. We integrate the Y's principles of character development—honesty, caring, respect, and responsibility—with building healthy relationships. These four principles, in addition to safety, are the foundation of everything we do.

"We're going to give out $80,000 in scholarships this year to those who need them, all on money raised from anonymous donors who want to send a kid to camp.

"And although the Y was formed as the 'Young Men's Christian Association,' that has nothing to do with the composition of our membership today. There are no barriers of color, sex, race, or religion. The Y is for *anyone* who wants to join."

CAMP MANAGEMENT

Bob Campbell has this to say to anyone interested in a YMCA camping career: "A passion for kids and the desire to make a positive difference in their lives is the most important consideration. After that it's on-the-job training. Experience in a camp setting can never be experienced in a classroom. So anyone interested needs to get involved as much as possible—as an employee, volunteer, intern, or whatever—to fully understand what it takes and what to expect."

At Sherman Lake, approximately 12 full-time paid staff members work directly in the program areas. Another 12 part-time Recreation Center workers greet members, process memberships, and work the various desks. Campbell hires more than 90 people for the summer programs, and another 16 to work on the spring and fall programs. If a YCMA camping career interests you, talk to someone at your local Y for information about the nearest camp in your area.

A Person Who's Done It

MEET BOB CAMPBELL

VITAL STATISTICS

Two strong role models put Bob Campbell on the path to a career of counseling and camp management. One was his dad, who was in the YMCA for 35 years and gave Bob his first camping job. The other was Bruce Iverson, an older friend and camp counselor who became the brother Bob never had. Beginning when Bob was ten years old, he was pretty much Bruce's shadow at camp, the better to become as good a camper as Bruce was. As it happened, this strategy couldn't have worked better.

I think my desire to get into camping goes all the way back to my first camping experience at a Lutheran church camp when I was nine or ten years old. Bruce Iverson, a counselor there, pretty much changed my life, as far as helping me decide what I wanted to do. I followed Bruce everywhere, and tried to be exactly like him. He seemed to know everything, and to do everything well. So when it came time for my dad to load up our blue '64 Ford station wagon to go home, I was devastated when I realized that Bruce wasn't coming with us, and I lost it. I cried the whole eight-hour drive home.

Years later when I was about 20, which was Bruce's age when he counseled me, I had a chance to return the favor. It was my first summer of counseling, and Bruce brought both his daughter Erica and his son Adam to our camp. It was a breathtaking experience to know that I'd be counseling *his* children, just as he had counseled me ten years before that!

I got my first camp job at age 16 as a ranch hand in South Dakota, and pretty much stayed in camping every summer until I was 22, as a counselor or recreation director. I got my first YMCA professional job at the Oshkosh, Wisconsin, Y as day camp director, where my dad was the executive director. Five years later I was recruited to be full-time resident director at Camp Nan-A-Bo-Sho in the Appleton, Wisconsin, YMCA where I stayed for seven years. Then in 1998 I was invited to interview at Sherman Lake for the director of camping services opening, and I got it. They were going through a national search, and had just started their resident camp program. I'm very proud to be part of this new venture. Today we're a state-of-the-art, fully operational, year-round camp. We raised $13 million to make it happen in three phases, two of which are complete. The third phase is a 20,000-square-foot leadership development lodge that we hope ultimately to use, at least in part, to train young people who are interested in making a career in the Y.

I've been in and out of college, first majoring in music and then in human services, as I figured out what I wanted to do with my life. But I realize that if I want to become an executive director, I need a college degree. The Y has great scholarship and grant programs for employees who want to get to the executive level, which I will try to utilize. So I know this is not beyond my reach financially.

But at any level, people who want to do this kind of work have to be sure they are committed to kids, and not worry about the money. It's a time-consuming job, but there are great benefits and plenty of time off for my family. You might say I'm in this for the long run.

JOBS, JOBS, JOBS

Says Paul Katz, director of YMCA relations: "Probably more than any other not-for-profit organization in the country—and the Y is the largest, both in membership and in funding—there is a commitment to provide opportunities for young people.

"And there are lots of opportunities in the Y for high school grads—both men and women—who have an interest in health and wellness," says Katz. "Many Ys have fitness facilities for kids, and they're hiring young people who can more readily relate to teenagers to work in the weight and exercise rooms.

"Right now we can't find enough people to fill the available jobs. In 1999 we had about 14,000 paid professional staff, and we expect that figure to grow to 25,000 within the next ten years. Each Y is an independent corporation and sets it own policies and pay scales, so both the programs and what they cost is pretty much determined by community needs and standards. Across the board there is a need for:

- Trainers

- Exercise room supervisors

- Equipment trainers

- Trainer supervisors

- Aquatic directors

- Lifeguards

- SCUBA instructors

"Another track is that young person who is interested in teaching sports to preschoolers, school-age kids, and middle school kids." (To learn more about the variety of YMCA career opportunities available, call (800) 872-9622, or spend some time on the Y web site: *www.ymca.net*.)

The Y philosophy is to strongly encourage employee professional growth to positions of greater responsibility. "There is scholarship and grant money available for both education and training programs," says Paul Katz.

"Springfield College maintains seven campuses around the country. We can program both bachelor's and graduate degrees for senior directors, depending on the situation. Some of these scholarship programs target minority staff members. Others are more generic."

YMCA SCUBA PROGRAM INSTRUCTORS AND DIVERS

National dive training in the United States began with the development of the YMCA SCUBA program. The first instructors were certified in Chicago in 1959. They established a standard of diver safety and proficiency that exists today. It has led to their training divers throughout the world, as well as helping to form other diving organizations.

In 1980 YMCA SCUBA became a federation of the *Confédération Mondiale des Activités Subaquatiques* (CMAS), or World Underwater Federation, the only world-recognized diving organization. This means that Y-trained divers and instructors are awarded the following CMAS benefits:

• Global acceptance and international recognition

• Ability to dive in countries where authorization is needed

• Ability to rent equipment and refill cylinders abroad

• Ease in joining international diving groups

You need to be at least 15 years old to take the YMCA SCUBA course, which includes approximately 32 hours of training in classroom, pool, and open water. All you need to begin is a mask, snorkel, and fins. Y instructors provide either all or most of the other equipment and materials, depending on the location. If there is no instructor in your area, you can find one on the web site below, or by calling YMCA SCUBA headquarters director Tec Clark or one of his assistants in Norcross, Georgia. The toll-free number is (888) 464-9622; the e-mail address is *scubaymca@aol.com*.

The completion of this course is essential for anyone interested in becoming a SCUBA instructor. Beyond this, a candidate must be 18 years of age or older and complete a three-phase training sequence. Following are *a few* of the requirements for each of the three phases. If you are interested in learning more, the entire three-phase instructor program is described on the Y web site: *www.ymcascuba.org*, or at the nearest YMCA to conduct instructor courses.

DIVEMASTER

A certified YMCA Divemaster is qualified to provide on-site leadership for groups of certified divers during recreational SCUBA diving, or for students during training, under the direct supervision of a YMCA SCUBA instructor. The Divemaster in Training course consists of 40 or more hours of training time. To enter the program a candidate must be at least 18 years of age, and have logged 20 dives, including night dives, navigation dives, and search and recovery diving.

ASSISTANT INSTRUCTOR

Assistant Instructors may be used in all aspects of classroom and pool training during the Open Water Diver course, under the direct supervision of a YMCA SCUBA instructor. To enter the program a candidate must be at least 18 years old, have completed Divemaster training or an approved equivalent from a recognized agency, have logged at least 30 dives, have Rescue Diver certification, and be certified in SCUBA Lifesaving Accident Management (SLAM).

SILVER SCUBA INSTRUCTOR

The Instructor certification qualifies an individual to teach SCUBA students to become competent divers. The instructor should also develop SCUBA leadership by instructing Divemasters and Assistant Instructors. To enter the program a candidate must have completed requirements or be certified as a SCUBA Assistant Instructor, and have a minimum of 60 logged dives, including at least five from the following list:

- 10 dives to greater than 80 feet (24 m)

- 10 dives utilizing full wet suit, including hood and gloves

- 10 dives utilizing minimal thermal protection (dive skin or shorty)

- 10 night dives

- 10 dives of less than 3 feet (.91 m) visibility

- 10 freshwater dives

- 10 saltwater dives

- 10 dives in surf, drift, or current conditions

- 4 diving specialty certifications

THE RIGHT STUFF

"I think what makes Y instructors different," says Gold Instructor Beth Dalzell, "is that all the rest of the SCUBA agencies are for profit. That doesn't mean that we don't want to make money when we teach, but we stick with the Y philosophy of Mind, Spirit, and Body in our teaching. We share what's in the mind, through the intelligence. Sharing the Spirit is sharing the love of the sport. You'll work your tail off to help make a student succeed, even those most frustrated with their progress. Body is the physical part; you're underwater, and you're sharing your skills as best you can.

"We do recognize that sometimes people make mistakes," says Dalzell. "And if you make a mistake, you need to know how to get out of it. We teach students how to fix the problem. Basically, our goal is to make divers so comfortable in the water that if something does go wrong they can react to it both calmly and efficiently.

"I think the best instructors have a willingness to learn, an ability to put their egos second, an awareness that individuals learn different skills at different speeds and in different ways, and a capacity to give of themselves."

A Person
Who's Done It

MEET BETH DALZELL

VITAL STATISTICS

Beth Dalzell didn't want to be a SCUBA instructor. Her primary interest was finding a hobby to enjoy on weekends. In fact, it was five years after being certified as a YMCA SCUBA diver that she even thought about teaching the sport. Today, Beth coordinates Y SCUBA instruction in eleven eastern states and is a full-time special education teacher as well. She wouldn't think of doing anything else.

I've always been around water. I could swim before I could walk. As a kid I spent most of my summers on the Jersey shore, in Beach Haven. My summer friends were closer to me than my winter friends because when we were in school, starting in April we'd be down there every weekend until the end of October.

So I was really water-oriented. My dad was a fisherman, and always loved it. I used to watch *Sea Hunt* with Lloyd Bridges on a regular basis. (Of course if kids today haven't seen the reruns, they won't ever have heard of it.) That was my all-time favorite show. And I also used to watch Jacques Cousteau underwater specials. So, underwater was the place that I really wanted to be. My father would swim in the ocean with me, but my mother was scared to death of it; she would go in, but she was always nervous about it.

Years later, after I was married, I heard about a course at the YMCA in Montclair, New Jersey, that was affordable, and I took it. My husband wasn't interested in taking it, so I just decided to go ahead because I'd probably never have anyone else to do it with, anyway.

It was a 12-week course, one night a week, an hour to an hour and a half in the class each time, and up to two hours in the pool. I loved it. I hooked up with some of the teaching assistants who were helping with the course, who also belonged to a New Jersey dive club. They were all very wonderful, giving people. Every one of them was a volunteer for that course. I joined the club, and found out I had people to dive with. I started diving right away. I took an advanced course, where I learned how to dive in the ocean from a dive boat. And I ended up diving every weekend.

It was great. I learned how to catch lobsters, and bring mussels home, and find scallops. I didn't do fish because I don't like to stab them, and I don't like to shoot guns. Because I wanted to stay informed, I went as a volunteer, and continued helping with classes. They kept saying, "Take the AI [Assistant Instructor] course." I never wanted to be a SCUBA instructor. All I wanted to do was help with the classes so I could stay in touch with everything, but finally I agreed. And once I became an AI, my friends talked me into taking the Instructor's course. So now I'm a Gold SCUBA Instructor, which essentially means that I've been an instructor for at least three years, and have certified at least 50 open water students over that period. You also have to have picked up a certain number of specialty certifications, and staff some of the leadership training programs.

Our certification is as good as you can get. I'll show my basic card when I'm diving on vacation, and over and over I hear, "Oh, she's a YMCA diver. She's OK." I never show my Instructor's card, though, because invariably I'll be asked to team up with a weak diver. That's where I draw the line; I'm on vacation, and I don't want the liability—or the hassle.

I had a student who did very well through the entire class, and when she got to the open water checkout dive, something happened to her and she couldn't go. She was on her way down the line and she freaked out. We sent her back to the beach, and she sat there disgusted with herself while the rest of us went down. Then I came out and sat at the water's edge with her, and asked if she'd like to just put the tank on one more time, and she agreed. At the quarry where we did a dive, the wall kind of slides away, and divers aren't aware of the water's depth if they're not looking at their gauges. So we just slid along the wall, equalizing every few minutes, as you're supposed to, and before long we were down to 30 feet (9 m), where the platforms were. She had no idea, and of course was elated. And it was all because she was willing to take that second chance.

It's times like these that I know I'm doing my job. Especially when a student says to me after finishing my class, "You should charge a whole lot more, because you give so much." That feels good.

GETTING IN AND MOVING UP

If you're a certified diver and want to be an instructor, according to Beth Dalzell, the best way to see if you'd like this job is to work in a dive shop during vacations—any dive shop. "Other than that," says Beth, "if someone in my class says, 'I really want to do what you do,' I say, 'That's great' and I mentor them by teaching them the skills as well as the physics behind all of our instruction. They learn the laws—Boyle's Law, Dalton's Law, Archimedes' Principle, Henry's Law—but only as the laws affect their lives when they're underwater.

"What I expect of anyone who wants to become a SCUBA instructor," says Beth, "is to assist me in all my classes. I want my instructor candidates to be my sidekicks through the full 12-week course, to follow everything that I do, to question me when they don't understand what I'm doing, and to make suggestions when it occurs to them; I can learn from them as well as teach them. Then, during the second 12-week course they may begin to volunteer parts of the instruction, either in class or in the pool. And this is all before they even enroll for the AI course.

"As a YMCA SCUBA instructor you have the opportunity to teach specialty courses, not just the basic courses. So, provided you're well prepared, you can teach wreck diving, underwater photography, underwater navigation, archeology, and courses for people with disabilities who still want to dive, such as those with asthma.

"I don't want to glamorize the job. It's tough to make money at it. It's a lot of physical work, because you're lugging heavy equipment, and you have to maintain the equipment that you are lugging. The teaching is mostly done in the evenings, because people work during the day to pay for the course. But if all that doesn't bother you, it's the most gratifying thing you'll ever do."

A FEW KEY POINTS TO REMEMBER

• Although the financial rewards from working at public service organizations usually are less than in the private sector, the work can be deeply satisfying.

• The number of paid professional staff is expected to grow from 14,000 to 25,000 within the next ten years.

• Scholarship and grant money is available from the YMCA to aid in completing training programs for positions with increased responsibility.

• What to learn from Bob: (1) The Y is for anyone who wants to join, regardless of race, sex, color, or religion; (2) Most Y camping programs integrate the principles of character development (honesty, caring, respect, responsibility) with building healthy relationships.

• What to learn from Beth: The best SCUBA instructors have a willingness to learn, an ability to put their egos second, an awareness that individuals learn different skills at different speeds, and a capacity to give of themselves.

CHAPTER FOUR

Careers In, On, and Near the Water

Of the ten most popular sports and fitness activities pursued by Americans—based on the table on pages 3–4 of Chapter One—three are closely tied to water. One hundred million people swim, snorkel, or SCUBA dive on either a regular or recreational basis. Add fishing and the paddle sports of kayaking, canoeing, and whitewater rafting, and you get 184 million, more than half the population of the United States.

What's going on here? Well, this figure doesn't take into account the fact that most people participate in more than one outdoor activity, so every one of those people is being counted two, three, or four times, depending on how many sports or activities they enjoy. Other water-related activities yet to crack the top ten, but all being enjoyed more widely today than they were five years ago, include diving, water polo, long-distance swimming, and water skiing.

AQUATICS DIRECTOR

For anyone with an interest in swimming so highly developed that a professional life beckons, there is a fairly well-prescribed route to more challenging positions. It begins with training to be a lifeguard, then pool supervisor, and finally aquatics director. (Larger programs may also require an assistant director.) Jobs exist in a variety of places: public and private fitness centers and health clubs, cruise ships and resorts, public and private golf and tennis clubs, and city and county parks departments. In the northern part of the country, where only outdoor pools are usually available, this still will be a summer job only, and you'll need to find winter work to stay employed year-round.

WHAT AQUATIC DIRECTORS DO

In a year-round facility, such as that at the Farmington, New Mexico, Parks and Recreation Department, Aquatics Director Patty Moran supervises as many as 50 lifeguards during the summer, and 20 to 25 during the winter. Her full-time staff consists of an assistant director, an office coordinator, a maintenance technician, and a pool supervisor. Two indoor pools and one outdoor pool comprise the Farmington aquatic system.

"In the summer we run five two-week sessions," says Patty Moran, "each with anywhere from 200 to 250 kids. It's a very popular program. We offer fourth-grade swimming lessons for all the grade schools in Farmington, as part of the curriculum. So for three weeks, instead of going to gym class, the kids get in a bus and go to one of the city pools. We also have programming for adults: exercise classes, lap swimming, adult lessons, and competitive swimming."

Every facility with an extensive swimming program—city recreation department, cruise ship, corporate fitness center—needs a competent aquatics director. The larger the program, the more qualified people are needed. The Geneva Glen Camp, in Indian Hills, Colorado, recently posted its requirements for the position, as well as for the job of pool head, or top assistant to the aquatics director. Here is what they are looking for to fill the top position (requirements will vary depending on the type of facility):

AQUATICS DIRECTOR

Minimum Qualifications

- Training and experience in pool and swimming activities
- Current certifications appropriate to position (water safety instructor, lifeguard, etc.)
- Current CPR and first aid certifications
- Knowledge of pool management
- Ability to schedule and supervise staff
- Desire and ability to work with children
- Good character, integrity, and adaptability
- Enthusiasm, sense of humor, patience, and self-control
- At least 19 years of age

General Responsibility

To plan, direct, and supervise camp's swimming program

Specific Responsibilities

Supervise the Pool Director to:

- set up pool area during staff orientation
- teach staff their responsibilities during staff orientation
- conduct initial and end of season inventory, and store equipment for safety
- conduct daily check of equipment for safety, cleanliness, and good repair
- evaluate aquatic abilities of staff and campers
- ensure that chemical levels in pool are correct and safe
- record all chemical levels, and test pool water twice daily
- submit orders for necessary equipment and supplies; ensure timely delivery
- assist in packing all materials and supplies at end of season
- evaluate current season and make suggestions for following season
- fulfill all requirements as counselor to assigned cabin or dorm

Essential Functions

- Ability to swim and teach swimming
- Ability to act quickly in case of emergency
- Ability to maintain pool facility in safe proper condition, meeting all health regulations
- Ability to supervise campers and staff in water
- Ability to implement and enforce pool safety and cleanliness rules

WHAT THE JOB IS *REALLY* LIKE

"This job is hectic during the summer," says Patty Moran, "but in a way it's even more challenging in the winter. We have to do a lot of promoting of the facility, a lot of budgetary work, some conflict resolution with the staff. Also, I'm instructor for the water safety instructors. They have to be 17 years old to qualify, and take a 40-hour class to qualify for certification.

"There's a lot of program planning and evaluating. During the winter I get here about 8:00 A.M., and if someone is out I may open earlier. I leave between 5:00 and 6:00 P.M., unless I have a meeting. I have my cell phone with me, so basically I'm on call 24 hours a day, 7 days a week. In the summer I come in at 7:00 A.M. and stay for the evening program.

"Unfortunately, some of the parents see us as baby-sitters for their three-to five-year-olds. They get upset that we don't allow their children to wear water wings, so they can run errands while we teach their children to swim."

A Person Who's Done It

MEET PATTY MORAN

VITAL STATISTICS

Patty Moran's career at the Farmington, New Mexico, Parks and Recreation Department started by chance when she decided to take swimming lessons at the town pool. Let's let her tell the story of how the friendship she developed with the aquatics director eventually led to her getting the job herself.

I had just moved to Farmington, and one day, when I went to the pool with my niece, I struck up a conversation with the aquatics director (although that may not have been her actual title), and decided to take swimming lessons. It was easy to get involved; I was 23 at the time and quite motivated. So then I took the water safety instructor class, which is a step toward becoming a lifeguard.

By this time it was August and I had become friends with the aquatics director. She asked if I would like to start working, and I agreed.

At first I just worked as a lifeguard part time, because I was also taking some college classes. Then in January the director offered me a full-time position, and I accepted it. Two years later I was promoted to pool supervisor.

About ten years ago my boss retired, and I took her place. Actually, she was my mentor and had groomed me for the position.

We had a great base program already, so what I've tried to do is increase the level of participation. I've geared the smaller pool toward more adult exercises. It's a homier atmosphere, and a lot of our older patrons seem to like that. We've also started kayaking and SCUBA programs. Anybody interested can learn in the pool, and then hone their skills on the nearby rivers or lakes.

In all three pools we've tried to create a strong swimming lesson program. In the summer we run five sessions, each with anywhere from 200 to 250 kids, for two weeks. It's a very popular program. We also have a large home school population in Farmington, so we've scheduled programs for those kids in the morning when the other pupils are in school.

Every fourth-grader in Farmington takes swimming lessons as part of the physical education curriculum, and at no cost to the kids; all the school district pays for is the bussing. There are children who would never have had the opportunity to learn to swim without this three-week program.

One great bonus for me started when I began teaching a class of older people; they must have been in their fifties. We had a wonderful time, and they were very nice to me. I've become good friends with a number of them, and I think at that point I realized that I had an opportunity to make a real difference in people's lives. So I've gone back to school, and shortly I'll get my bachelor's degree in social work. I've decided to take early retirement in three and a half years, and I particularly want to work in geriatrics.

As far as opportunities for high school grads are concerned, our pool supervisor and lifeguard positions do not require a college education. Once they turn 18, our lifeguards are eligible to apply for supervisory positions. It's a good opportunity to work your way up. We use a lot of on-the-job training. I encourage the young people to take college courses on supervision, or anything else that could help them move into positions of more responsibility. These days, most people who have my position also have a college degree. More and more often, this is the case.

WHITEWATER INSTRUCTORS AND GUIDES

"We're in a different business today than when I first got here in 1983," says Russell Walters, president of Northern Outdoors, in The Forks, Maine. "In those days it was a summer business only. People would come here to raft or kayak during the day, and sleep under the stars or find a motel someplace at night.

"Nowadays it's more formal and less spontaneous. People want a year-round program. We had to find a way to make it work in winter as well as summer, which is why we developed a winter snowmobile program, and a professional, year-round staff. It's a very aggressive business."

Northern Outdoors is the largest facility of its kind in northern New England, set on more than 100 acres of woods on the shores of the Kennebec River. Among its year-round range of activities are whitewater rafting, sport kayaking, rock climbing, snowmobiling, hunting, freshwater fishing, kayak tours, and a ropes course. Its amenities include lakeside log cabins, a deluxe lodge, riverside campsites, a heated pool, hot tubs, restaurant, lounge, and a brew pub.

A Person Who's Done It

MEET RUSSELL WALTERS

VITAL STATISTICS

As a boy growing up in Windsor, England, Russell Walters kayaked and canoed on the River Thames. It was his favorite thing to do. Years later, after graduating from high school, Russell was fascinated at the sight of his first Maine whitewater river, pictured in a U.S. travel book. From then on it was only a matter of time—and some ingenuity—until he was given a tryout as a kayak guide at Northern Outdoors. Today he is the company's president. Russell tells his story:

From the age of seven, I spent all of my spare time in a kayak or a canoe. It was my favorite sport. When I saw that picture of real U.S. white water, my first reaction was "Wow! To be able to play and train on wild, free-flowing rivers like that would be great!" The Thames, where I paddled, was pretty, but it was also flat and boring.

At about the same time I had a chance to talk with friends of mine, who were three or four years older than I, and members of the British kayak racing team. They had stopped in the States after competing in the world championships in Canada, and some U.S. team members took them to the Kennebec River (a few miles from here!) for some fun. It blew them away, and when I heard about it, I decided I wasn't going to waste any more summers on the Thames. After a couple of years I was selected to be on the British team.

British and American kayakers are very different, by the way. The Brits are very structured, with tremendous technical skills but limited natural resources. Instructors can pull apart any stroke sequence, and analyze it from a technical aspect. The Americans had all these wild and free-flowing rivers to practice on, but limited access to technical coaches. So it was a wash.

To get over here I sent a letter to every river outfitter I knew about in the Northeast; I think there were 13 of them at the time. I let them know I was a member of the British team, that I was certified to teach kayaking, that I didn't need to be employed full-time. Essentially, all I needed was a bed, and didn't have to be paid very much! Northern Outdoors was the only one of the 13 to respond. The deal we worked out was that they would give me $75 a week, plus room and board. If I was any good, I could stay. If I was not good, they would pay my way out of here.

As it turned out, I liked them and they liked me. After a couple of years I was promoted to marketing manager, and a few years later to president. A West Coast job lured me to California for a few years, but I wasn't able to stay away for long. I think I'm here for a while. Down the road I may think about a marketing venture, but for now I like what I'm doing.

GETTING IN AND MOVING UP

With a year-round staff, Walters is strongly committed to cross-training. The chances of employment for young people just out of high school are excellent. "We don't pigeonhole our staff," he says. "Most essential is a willingness to learn and be part of the team, and a genuine liking for people. Our river guides have to be 21 before we ever start to train them, because there's a certain level of maturity that is required. Let me give you an example:

"Jeremy, a young fellow who was hired as a housekeeper, came up and sat next to me on the deck one day, and said, 'Russell, do you know what I really want to do? Be a river guide. But I don't have the money to go through the training.'

"I said, 'Jeremy, we can make that happen for you, but the problem is that then you will want to become a guide, and you have a commitment to housekeeping.'

"'No,' said Jeremy. 'I'll work in housekeeping five days a week, and work as a guide for one, through this year. Then if I prove myself, Id like to come on as a guide.'

"That's how it worked out. Jeremy is now a guide, and he's unbelievable. He'll do things that other people coming in here would not consider doing. Also, he can make beds! It's so valuable for us to have someone like a waiter or waitress who can also talk about being on the river, and then make it happen."

Cindy McLaughlin, beginning her eighth year, is another example of the Northern Outdoors cross-training policy. "I was 20 when I first came on board, and started at the front desk," she says. "The next year I became a shift supervisor in the office, and at the same time graduated from our whitewater guide school. The year after that I trained as a ropes course facilitator."

Today, Cindy's primary responsibility is as Northern Outdoors' sales manager, dealing with $3 to $4 million in reservations each year. "But I'm still able to take a group on a whitewater rafting trip," she says, "or spend a day rock climbing with the guests.

"I think the best part of all is reading e-mails from the guests after they get home, and knowing we did a good job by hearing how much they enjoyed themselves."

NORTHERN OUTDOORS EMPLOYMENT FORECAST

Here are the employment opportunities currently available at Northern Outdoors, all within reach of motivated high school graduates:

- Reservations/Sales Staff

- Group Sales Coordinator

- Wait Staff

- Front Desk/Guest Service

- Housekeeping

- Grounds

- Maintenance

- Fishing Guide

- Whitewater Guide

- Recreational Guide (kayaking, overnight adventures, hiking, many others)

- Hunting Guide

- Snowmobile Trail Groomer

- Accountant/Bookkeeper

- Bartender

- Security

- Videographer/Photographer

- Bus Driver/Shuttle Driver

- Chef/Cook

- Receptionist

- Ropes Course/Team Building Facilitator

- Rock Climbing Instructor

For more information about jobs with river and lake outfitters, visit the following web sites:

- **The American Whitewater Affiliation** (*www.americanwhitewater.org*)
  In operation to conserve and restore America's whitewater resources and to enhance opportunities to enjoy them safely. Has links to information regarding membership, resources, rivers, publications, conservation, and affiliates.

- **Cool Works—Jobs in Great Places**
  (*www.coolworks.com/jobs-on-water.htm*)
  Extensive list of ocean, river, and beach jobs in national parks, camps, ranches, state parks, resorts, ski areas, and on cruise lines. Jobs listed by state, including volunteer work.

- **Canoeing and Kayaking Information by Paddling.Net**
  (*www.paddling.net*)
  Locate guides, outfitters, and rental facilities anywhere in North America. Includes paddling schools, paddling news (from a conservation point of view), and upcoming events.

- **Northern Outdoors** (*www.northernoutdoors.com*)
  More details about what you've read in this chapter—action pictures, too!

SYNCHRONIZED SWIMMING COACH

It took nearly 80 years for synchronized swimming to go from an "underwater ballet," at New York's Hippodrome, to Tracie Ruiz and Candy Costie's gold medal duet performance at the 1984 XXIII Olympiad in Los Angeles.

That event marked the first time millions of people had ever seen this intricate and teamwork-centered sport performed.

Nancy Wightman, assistant athletic director at Keuka College in the Finger Lakes district of New York, has been involved in synchronized swimming since high school; she is head coach of the sport at Keuka, and the sport's representative to the Olympic Committee. "Actually there are six levels of coaches," says Wightman. "I'm at Level V. National team coaches are Level VI.

"I was a 'pool rat' back in California, and had gone through all the Red Cross levels. They didn't know what to do with me. Finally one of the instructors said, 'Get over here and help teach these little kids to swim'; so that's what I did. I was 13. Then I put on a water show in high school, which was my introduction to synchronized swimming—and I was hooked. I took courses in college, and started teaching it when I was a grad student."

Interested students with synchronized swimming experience can become certified coaches at age 16.

Other Level I prerequisites are

• Current U.S. Synchronized Swimming (USSS) membership

• Current certification in:
  Adult CPR
  Standard First Aid
  Safety Training for Swim Coaches
  or
  Lifeguard Training

Level I Course Requirements are

• Successful completion of Level I Coaching Certification Course

• Minimum score of 80 percent on written test covering course material

• At least ten hours of practice coaching, verified by USSS Certified Coach

The Level I course includes the following areas of coaching information:

- Basic Coaching Theory

- Coaching Ethics

- Risk Management

- Warmups and Workouts

- Strength, Flexibility, and Endurance

Requirements for higher coaching levels are understandably more demanding. For more information see the national organization's web site at *www.usasynchro.org*. Here you'll find complete information on membership and professional resources, and listings of open coaching jobs in this country and abroad; there were 14 such listings on a recent visit—"Coaches Wanted" link on the home page.

A Person Who's Done It

MEET NATHALIE BARTLESON

VITAL STATISTICS

For just about every one of her 14 years competing as an elite synchronized swimmer, Nathalie Bartleson felt like quitting. The demands on the rest of her life were almost more than she could manage, but she didn't give up, which probably is one big reason she achieved her sport's highest honor: a gold medal at the XXIII Olympiad in 1984. Here's her story.

I've been in the water since I was four. My mom says she taught me to swim in about a half hour. I had no swim team background, although I did have some ballet and a lot of energy, so at the age of nine I started swimming with the Walnut Creek team in California. We practiced two to four hours a day, first for three days a week, then after a couple of years, five and six days a week.

In synchronized swimming there is usually one coach for every eight to ten girls, until you get to the elite level. In addition to the coach, though, the athletes end up coaching one another, to act as additional eyes for the coach. It's really good to get this feedback, which is actually the way I learned to coach. Also, our coach would bring in other specialists. Once she brought in a swimming coach who worked on our strokes with us; her help made me one of the fastest swimmers on our team.

It seems as though I've always been an instructor or demonstrator. At 15 I coached little kids 10 and under. After a couple of years I coached 10-, 11-, and 12-year-olds. Then later I helped coach our own top-level teams.

At some point all of this concentrated work began to catch up with me. In those early teen years just before high school, kids want to do what everybody else is doing. Or if they don't get along with someone, it's tough—there's no place to go! So just about every year I wanted to quit, but it was never because I wasn't in love with the sport, so I'd stick it out one more year. Also, I had a single mom who couldn't pay for everything, so I had to find ways to make money, such as selling raffle tickets for team fund-raisers, baby-sitting, working at McDonald's, or waitressing. Still, having to pay for my activity actually made me appreciate it more.

It was in Australia at the World Aquatic Championships that I finally figured out the mental game. I relaxed, I reviewed my corrections, and I ended up being one of the top competitors in the compulsory competition. That's when I decided to go for the Olympics.

The experience was unbelievable. I can remember our performance clearly. I can also remember standing on the awards platform. I had to look down and wiggle my toes to make sure I wasn't dreaming.

I think synchronized swimming is an amazing endeavor for athletes, in that it teaches poise, teamwork, and taking initiative. It encourages coaches, as well, as they work with swimmers—to be organized, empathic, firm, and creative. As a coach, I feel privileged helping to develop the best in each athlete, as well as foster true team camaraderie and cooperation. Plus it's a free synchro show every day!

For anyone who wants to coach synchronized swimming, the information is easy to find. Just go to the web site (see page 62). If you want to start a synchronized swimming team, go to the local gymnastic or ballet schools, get a list of people who may want to consider an alternative, and recruit them.

You can make a good living coaching synchronized swimming, but if you want to coach at the college level, you'll have to get a degree, in many instances a graduate degree. Like all jobs, it's going to depend a lot on the time you want to put in.

FISHING GUIDE

Anyone who fishes outside familiar territory needs help to bring in the big ones, whether to eat, mount, or return to the water. Fishing guides make this happen, in all 50 states and for hundreds of kinds of fish. Fishing guides usually specialize, either by locale or by type of fish. For example, bass is very popular; of the first ten of *Fishing Guide's* "Top 35 Websites," five deal exclusively with bass fishing.

THE RIGHT STUFF

The most effective fishing guides combine the qualities of teacher, outdoorsman, pilot, entertainer, diplomat, and magician. James Hare, a guide in the Florida Keys, says a good memory helps, as well. "On the Keys you learn the territory by memorizing where dozens of mangrove islands are, as well as the occasional radio tower," says James.

"Actually, anyone who has passed the certification for a captain's license has had to absorb an incredible amount of information. The course I took was for seven hours a day, seven days, and on the eighth day we took the test. So far I've used only about 20 percent of the information we were tested on, but you never know."

WHAT FISHING GUIDES DO

"Down here we specialize in 'flats fishing,'" says James, "which essentially is fishing in very shallow water. The areas range in depth from a few inches to several feet—up to 10 feet (3 m) if you're tarpon fishing. It's very tide-dependent. The fish come up to feed from deeper water to the flats as the tide is going out.

"Finding the fish under these circumstances can be difficult, because there are so many variables. Guides study for decades before they're considered really good at it. I was down here for a year before getting my captain's license, just to learn some of the places to which I could take people.

"Take wind speed, for example. If the winds are too high, the fish will change their habits. Not only that, the wind causes a chop that makes it difficult to see below the surface. When you're fly-fishing for tarpon, bonefish, permit, and barracuda, it's all sight-fishing; you have to be able to see the fish before you even cast the fly. So another main function of a guide is to find leeward areas in higher winds. This is tough when the wind changes as much as it does down here. Cloud cover can also wreak havoc with visibility.

"A typical day with a client starts the night before, when I prepare all my flies and leaders. Then at about 7:00 A.M., I tune my radio to NOAA (National Oceanic and Atmospheric Administration) for the weather. Despite the constant updates, there are so many microclimates down here that looking out the window can be just as effective; therefore, based on the weather forecast, the wind speed and direction, and the water temperature, I decide where I'm going to take my client.

"Then I prepare the boat. I check the fuel and other fluids, life jackets and other safety equipment, and food and water—I allow at least a gallon (3.8 L) per person. I take plenty of sun block, hats, and long-sleeved clothing; the sun is brutal.

"You have to be prepared for any contingency. You can enter a flat on an incoming tide, and find yourself scrambling to get to deeper water as the tide goes out. Water runs off the flats so quickly, and the flats are so large, that at low tide you could find yourself stranded out there. It's a terrifying experience, realizing that you could spend the next six hours waiting for the tide to free your boat. Also, it's no fun walking through the *marl* as you pull the boat off the flats. That stuff is like clay—it'll suck your shoes right off."

A Person Who's Done It

MEET JAMES HARE

VITAL STATISTICS

In 1996 James Hare and his brother Bill quit their New York jobs and moved to Cudjoe Key, Florida. Their intent was to take a year off, just to fish and kick back. After a year, Bill moved on, but James realized that the time he was spending on the water would be enough to qualify for a captain's license . . . so why not go for it?

I've been fishing since I was a kid, all over the country. So it seemed natural when the right time came along to do what I liked to do most—for a whole year! My brother loves fishing as much as I do, so we decided to just chuck everything for a year. We thought if we didn't do it then, we'd never do it.

It was great, although my brother tired of it before I did. I decided to stick it out, and followed through on my plan to become a licensed fishing guide. My initial plan was to work for eight or nine months, and then take off for Montana to guide on the trout streams when the fishing died down here. I haven't been able to manage that yet.

I bought a boat and figured out the overhead, and thought I could make it work. The idea of taking people out and doing what I loved to do anyway had a huge appeal to me. Good guides charge $350 to $450 per day, plus tip. I charged $250 for a half day, $350 for a full day.

What I didn't realize was that fish guiding would be so highly competitive. I can see where they're coming from. It's taken these guys years to earn the knowledge that makes them as good as they are, and they don't want to give it away to competitors. I mean, there's no open hostility; in fact, most of the guys are quite cordial. It's just that you aren't going to get a straight answer from them if it means giving up some hard-earned information.

Someday I'd like to be able to offer a more versatile service. Some people, for example, are more interested in what's happening ecologically than in fishing all day. It's a rich and diverse area, but there are also problems. It's also just great sightseeing. I can take people places where a spotted eagle ray or an 8-foot (2-m) shark will pass under the boat—just 4 feet (1.2 m) below us! I know where the spiny lobsters are, and the best coral reefs for snorkeling.

Anyway, I can't think of a better life—at least for me. I make my own hours, and even if I don't work a five-day week, I can make a good living. Best of all, while I'm working I'm also playing.

USEFUL WEB SITES

- **Fishing Guides Home Page** (*www.thumpersgraphics.com*)
  Freshwater fishing guides, saltwater fishing charters, and fly-fishing guides from all 50 states and around the world. Links to hundreds of other fishing-related sites, national and local weather listings, and discussion boards (on which to look for jobs and post résumés).

A FEW KEY POINTS TO REMEMBER

- There are a number of career opportunities in water-related sports, which can be found in fitness centers, on cruise ships, and at resorts, public and private golf and tennis clubs, and city and county parks departments.

- What to learn from Patty: (1) There is great satisfaction in teaching people a sport that makes a real difference in their lives. (2) Pool supervisor and lifeguard positions do not require college educations. There is a lot of on-the-job training and good opportunity to work your way up.

- Outfitters are a rapidly growing industry. There are numerous entry-level job opportunities for those interested in whitewater rafting, kayaking, rock climbing, snowmobiling, and freshwater fishing.

- What to learn from Russell: (1) The job market for high school graduates is excellent. (2) Most important is a willingness to learn and to be part of a team.

- What to learn from Nathalie: (1) A love for a sport can keep you going—don't quit! Learn to relax. (2) You can make a good living coaching synchronized swimming, but you need a degree to coach at the college level.

- What to learn from James: (1) A good fishing guide must be part teacher, part outdoorsman, part pilot, part entertainer, part diplomat, and part magician. (2) A good fishing guide must be prepared for all contingencies.

CHAPTER FIVE

Careers Uphill, Downhill, and on the Field

A fire in the potbelly wood stove takes some of the chill from a cool autumn afternoon as Daq Woods tightens the screw of a vise holding a twisted bicycle wheel. Sighting along the rim, Daq removes a badly bent spoke as he talks about his job at West Hill Shop, in Putney, Vermont.

"It's rewarding to be able to fix things," Daq says. "I'll get a little kid in here with a bike that's been backed over by a car—like this one—and his parents will tell me, 'I doubt if you can fix this, but please try because he sure loves his bike.' Being able to call up that family a few days later to tell them the bike is ready, and finally seeing the look on the kid's face when it turns out to be as good as new . . . well, there's not a much better feeling than that."

WHAT BIKE AND SKI SHOP WORKERS DO

The retail sales part of what Daq does includes assisting customers in finding what they are looking for and trying to interest them in buying the merchandise. Salespeople describe a product's features and demonstrate its use. Many, if not most, bicycle and ski shop salespeople are proficient in one or both sports themselves, and are thus better able to describe ways various features of a product are best utilized.

In addition to selling, retail salespeople make out sales checks; receive cash, checks, and charge payments; bag or package purchases; and give change and receipts. They may also help stock shelves or racks, arrange for mailing or delivery of purchases, mark price tags, take inventory, and prepare displays.

Those workers who also specialize in bicycle repair must be able to diagnose problems and determine the best way to solve them. They obtain supplies and repair parts from distributors. They use common hand and power tools, as well as specialized equipment. They replace or fix worn or broken parts, where necessary, or make adjustments. Those who work in small establishments often do all of the repairs, and work under minimal supervision. As you might suspect, the pay scale for skilled bike mechanics is considerably higher than for a sales clerk.

A BIKE SHOP/SKI OUTLET

Like many bike shops in four-season areas, West Hill Shop in Putney, Vermont, becomes a Nordic and back-country ski outlet sometime between Halloween and Thanksgiving, meaning that employees must become familiar with both sports, and give equally useful advice about two completely different seasonal product lines. Like many quality shops, West Hill prides itself on the service it offers owners of both the bikes it sells and the bikes it repairs. The shop maintains a clubhouse atmosphere by doubling as a gathering place for biking and cross-country ski fanatics in the area, some of whom hang out to talk about trails and equipment with founder and owner Neil Quinn and his staff. Those who can't stop by as often as they'd like check the Shop web site (*www.westhillshop.com*) to keep current, where they can find race results, schedules for training rides and night rides, occasional equipment deals, tips about training, fitness, and equipment, and weather conditions in the area. (Daq Woods drew the illustrations for the site.)

Neil Quinn has created the atmosphere that makes West Hill Shop more of a cycling or ski club than a retail store. Many of his former employees come back to say hello, and sometimes work again at the shop after 20 years or more doing other things in other places.

THE RIGHT STUFF

"When Neil first evaluated me for this job," says Daq, "he tried me out on a couple of bikes. What I guess he saw was that I got the idea, I paid attention to detail, was mechanically adept, and learned very quickly. These I think are the most important things."

Other qualities are important as well. Customers everywhere spend millions of dollars on merchandise, and often form their impressions of a store by evaluating its sales force. Retailers stress the importance of providing courteous and efficient service in order to remain competitive. When a customer wants an item that is not on the sales floor, for example, the salesperson may check the stockroom, place a special order, or call another store to locate the item.

Employers look for people who enjoy working with others and have the tact and patience to deal with difficult customers. Also desirable are an interest in sales work, a neat appearance, and the ability to communicate clearly and effectively. The ability to speak more than one language may be helpful in communities where people from various cultures live and shop. Before hiring a salesperson, some employers may conduct a background check, especially for a job selling high-priced items.

A typical day for Daq: "When I get here in the morning, I have a lot of things to do right away. I turn on the air compressor, so we can inflate the tires and blow dirt and dust off parts. Then I turn off the alarm, turn off the answering machine, turn on four computers, and move about 20 bikes outside for display.

"After that I go through my repair tickets. This tells me what the workload will be like for the day. I may have five bikes to work on; I may have ten. If I have ten and they're tough jobs that I don't think I can finish by myself, I call a good mechanic in Dummerston who comes in when we need him.

"About ten o'clock, when we open, Neil arrives and starts on his paperwork, doing orders, and answering the phone. Neil's son Bevan often comes in about then as well, to handle shipping and receiving, as well as some paperwork. He's also a mechanic, but he doesn't do as much of that as he used to.

"So I have bikes that need repair and I have customers coming in, and often I'll have a bike or two that needs to be assembled. The UPS truck shows up here five days a week. We're not the type of shop that orders 200 bikes during the preseason; we order them every week as we need them. Then at six we close, and everyone still here pitches in to see that things are turned off—or on—and that all the stock is back inside.

"Often by the time six o'clock rolls around, my body needs a release. Like any other job, when it gets busy here, life can be a little frustrating. But as I get older, I've learned to deal with the stress. You almost have to *practice* handling it. Anyway, it's times like these when I need a bike ride! I ride even in the dark; I have a great light. Since I moved up to Putney I only have a 4-mile (6.4-km) ride between home and work, so sometimes I get crafty and take a few trails that get the ride up to 8 miles (12.8 km) or so.

GETTING IN AND MOVING UP

Says Daq Woods: "This is a good career path for anyone getting out of high school who loves biking. For one thing, the deals you get are great. If I didn't work in this shop, I'd have to make big bucks to support my bicycle habit. I have six bikes and love every one of them."

Opportunities for advancement vary in small stores. Often, one person, usually the owner, does most of the managerial work. In others, however, some salespersons are promoted to assistant managers. More and more often, particularly in large retail businesses, college graduates are hired as management trainees, making a college education increasingly important. Despite this trend, motivated and capable employees without college degrees should still be able to advance to administrative or supervisory positions in large establishments.

A Person Who's Done It

MEET DAQ WOODS

VITAL STATISTICS

Daq Woods didn't wait until he graduated from high school to get into bicycle sales and maintenance. He's been doing what he loves for 15 years, and he's only 31. Here's how it happened:

It all started with my first bike. I guess I wore it out or something. In our barn were a bunch of old bike parts, so I'd start tinkering. I remember my mom saying, "You'd better not take that apart. You'll never get it back together." But somehow I always did.

One summer when I was about 14, I met an older kid named Bevan, whose father Neil owns this shop. We became friends riding bikes on the trails around Brattleboro. One day he came to my house. We went into my garage, where all my 13 million bike parts were laid out, and Bevan saw that I had built a rim. What I did was to dismantle all 36 spokes from a wheel, clean it, and put it back together. Each spoke has to weave over and under the other spokes in a certain pattern, and Bevan was impressed that I had done that by myself, without help, or reading a book, or anything. So he said, straight out, "Would you like to come work at my dad's shop?"

We rode up here from West Brattleboro, where we lived, about 12 miles away. (We had only one-speeds, but it was no big deal.) Neil put me to work on a couple of bikes to evaluate me, and it was apparent right away that I was mechanically adept, paid attention to detail, had the overall idea, and could learn very quickly, so he offered me a job! It was my first one, and it was a dream job. I was very excited.

When I was 15, I started working here. I'd either ride my bike or take the bus up here after junior high and work on bikes from three to six in the afternoon. I was a great mechanic from the get-go. They didn't have to give me a lot of training; I learned as I went.

It was really neat coming to this shop because it was different from all the other shops in the area. This place seemed to be about people who loved bikes; the others were more like showrooms.

EMPLOYMENT FORECAST

Opportunities for retail salespeople are expected to continue to be good because of the many job openings created each year, many to replace the large number of workers who transfer to other occupations or leave the workforce. There are always many opportunities for part-time workers, particularly during peak selling periods, such as the Christmas season. This is an ideal way to "try out" this kind of job, to see if it might be for you.

The hourly earnings of retail salespeople, including commission, averages about $7.75 nationwide; the middle 50 percent earn between $6.25 and $10.00 an hour, the lowest 10 percent earn about $5.50, and the highest 10 percent earn nearly $15 an hour.

JOBS IN SKI AND SNOWBOARD MOUNTAIN RESORTS

Every year in late September or early October, advertisements begin to appear for help in the ski resorts in the Northeast and West. Altogether, thousands of jobs become available, most of them seasonal but some of them full-time and permanent positions. Following are some of the positions that appeared in an ad posted by the Stratton Mountain Resort, in central Vermont, in the fall of 2000:

- Child Care Manager

- Rental Technicians

- Retail Sales Associates

- Ski/Snowboard Instructors

- KidsKamp Instructors

- Snowmakers

- Lift Attendants

- Cooks

- Groomers

- Reservation Agents

- Shuttle Drivers

- Housekeepers

- Custodians

- Front Desk Clerks

- Some year-round full-time positions available

And, as they say, "Much, much more." Use your favorite search engine to research possible jobs in your target locations. Try "Ski Resort Jobs," or other variations that may yield results, including specific resorts of interest to you.

SPORTS OFFICIALS

Soccer, lacrosse, hockey, and other sports officials are certified in accordance with qualification requirements determined by duly appointed committees, usually consisting partly of former officials themselves. Each candidate must pass both a physical as well as a written exam, verifying his or her mastery of the rules and fine points of the game.

Probably the fastest-growing of the major sports is soccer. Approximately 18 million people are soccer players at all levels—youth leagues, high school, college, amateur, and professional. From 1980 to 1995, youth soccer alone grew 336 percent. Having swept past baseball and football, it is now creeping up on basketball as the most popular game in the country.

As one consequence of soccer's phenomenal growth, referees are in great demand. Of the 11 referee grades, the first 4 (11 through 8) have no minimum age requirement. As a result, it is not uncommon to see 15- and 16-year-olds as associate referees, linesmen, and "Class 2" referees.

Vermont is one of a number of states that are short of referees. "The usual practice is to work a game with a senior official and a junior official," says Gunther Sihler, president of the Vermont Soccer Officials Association. "Because we don't have enough officials, often the senior person will get taken off an easy game for younger kids and put on a high school game.

"I'm also an assessor for high school and college games," says Sihler. "Assessors are assigned to observe soccer games and provide constructive feedback to the officials about what they can do to make their jobs easier. Many times when I'm assigned to assess a game there won't be enough refs, so I have to pitch in and ref instead. It's a vicious cycle."

A Person Who's Done It

MEET GUNTHER SIHLER

VITAL STATISTICS

You might say Gunther Sihler was born to be a soccer official. He's been doing it since he was 12, and in 1985, at age 17, he was the youngest high school soccer official in New York State—ever. Today as head of the Vermont Soccer Officials Association, Gunther plays two roles: as soccer official and as soccer association executive (he also is on the executive board of the New England Intercollegiate Soccer Officials Association). Oh yes, and one year he used his landscape architecture background to design sports arenas abroad.

Actually, I got into soccer officiating rather by accident. When I was 12 or 13, the father of a friend of mine was a high-level referee in the area, and he asked if I could fill in one day. I was a player, and thought it might be fun. In those days I lived and breathed soccer, and I guess my enthusiasm and love of the game made him think I would be a good official. Gradually I did more— playing and reffing at the same time. When I was a senior I began officiating high school games, which at age 17 made me the youngest referee ever to officiate a high school game.

I always thought I would spend more time as a player, then, as a University of Wisconsin freshman, I met a high-level referee who took me under his wing. It was full-time officiating through my senior year, mostly college-level games. Reffing helped pay my way through school.

Readers of this book should know that I could have been a soccer official whether I went to college or not. If you know the game well enough, love and respect it, and apply that knowledge and respect to the field with good decisions, you can be a good ref. A college degree doesn't have anything to do with it.

I took a break one year, going to Germany and designing sports arenas, but other than that, I've pretty much stayed in soccer. I was a downhill ski instructor for ten years. I also was director of a Vermont city parks and recreation department for two and one-half years, and assistant director in another city for more than three years.

What keeps me in this game, regardless of the level, is the enthusiasm I see. Winning a game and making a great shot or save is as important to a little kid as it is to a college student. Also, when I get in a challenging situation and am right on top of it to make the right call, that's a great feeling. But for pure excitement, I think working a championship game at the pro or college level is the greatest.

WHAT THE JOB IS *REALLY* LIKE

"When I was 12 or 13 just getting into officiating," says Gunther, "there was a lot of support for a young ref. That isn't true today. Now, people can be more abusive. You put a first-time ref on the field—either a boy or a girl, because there are more of both these days—and the coach is yelling; the players are yelling. After a year of it, some of these kids are saying, 'Who needs it?' Most of them are players, as well. They think, 'Why go on the field and ref a game if I can play instead?' We're trying to get more young people involved through mentoring programs and internships, but it's very difficult. Fifty percent of the entry-level refs who come in will not register next year. I'm sure the big reason for this is not just that they go out on the field and get yelled at. Part of it is their own personal situation."

GETTING IN AND MOVING UP

Soccer in the United States is *huge*; it's the coaching and the officiating that is lagging behind. To remedy this, soccer organizations are trying to make the system more professional, more user-friendly. They're identifying the young people who have potential, and bringing them through the ranks much more quickly. Their internship and mentoring programs allow them to put the best kids on a fast track.

A knowledgeable young kid can do well. In many states it's possible to officiate year-round and full time. And most of these younger officials are better officials, as well, because they have a natural respect and love of the game, which comes from having grown up playing it. Their understanding of soccer is natural, and not derived just from reading rule books.

Here are the best soccer and officiating sources:

- **U.S. Soccer On-Line** (*www.us-soccer.com*)
  Click the "Referee" icon in the menu upper-left. It will get you to everything from the U.S. Soccer Federation (USSF) referee e-magazine (*Fair Play*) to Laws of the Game. Also information on certification (including criteria for certifying and upgrading national referees), advice to referees, upcoming clinics, an entry-level referee training course, and the downloadable, 52-page *Referee Administrative Handbook*.

- **New England Intercollegiate Soccer Officials Association** (*www.nhsoccer.com*)
  A mega-site, of which the NEISOA is a small part. Links to NCAA, Youth Soccer, U.S. Adult Soccer, Online Coaching, Referee Pages, Major League Soccer, USSF, etc. (The home page runs 52 pages. Scroll through before downloading to see what might be worth saving.)

JOBS IN PUBLIC AND PRIVATE GOLF CLUBS

This country's 28 million golfers play more than a half billion rounds each year on some 15,000 courses, 80 percent of them public and 20 percent private. If you like golf, therefore, there are opportunities for you, on the course and in the clubhouse. Just remember that maintaining a golf course is like taking care of a 100- to 200-acre (405–810-sq-m) park.

City and county park and recreation departments often include golf courses, and are therefore good employment sources. For anyone interested in landscaping and lawn service, in addition to golf, the entry-level outside job most frequently available is greenskeeper or groundskeeper. If you are considering a golf-related career, you most likely have experience caddying at a local club. Talking to the club pro or the superintendent about entry-level opportunities at your club is probably the first place to begin. Inquire also about any internship possibilities.

GREENSKEEPERS

Greenskeepers make sure the underlying soil on fairways and greens has the required composition to allow proper drainage and to support the appropriate grasses used. They regularly mow, water, fertilize, and aerate the course. In addition, they apply chemicals and fungicides to control weeds, kill pests, and prevent diseases, and periodically relocate the holes on the putting greens to eliminate uneven wear of the turf and add interest and challenge to the game. They also keep canopies, benches, ball washers, and tee markers repaired and freshly painted.

Most states require certification for workers who apply pesticides. Certification requirements vary, but usually include passing a test on the proper and safe use and disposal of insecticides, herbicides, and fungicides.

SOURCES FOR JOBS IN GOLF COURSE MANAGEMENT

Most public and private golf courses, as well as recreation and park districts, maintain web pages, usually including a job opportunities corner. Look on a map to see what cities, towns, and private golf courses fall within the radius of an acceptable commute for you. You now have your universe of prospective employers. Contact them either by phone or by sending your résumé and an accompanying cover letter. (Read Chapters Seven and Eight for specific suggestions and strategies.) Because wages for beginners are low and the work is physically demanding, many employers have difficulty attracting enough workers to fill all openings.

Another source for jobs is the golf schools that offer game improvement lessons in more than 30 states. America's Favorite Golf Schools, for example, has outlets in 17 states alone. For a complete list, including addresses and phone numbers, check the Golf Course Management web site: *www.golfcoursemanagement.com.*

PROGRAMS

The Golf Course Superintendents Association of America offers a comprehensive set of programs for its members, all designed to provide a solid background in every component of the golf course management profession. These include financial management, media relations, and golf course renovation, among others. Through a student membership program, the GCSAA Foundation provides internship and scholarship possibilities for students pursuing careers in the golf course industry. Various sponsors award annual scholarships of from $500 to $3,500.

Students pursuing a four-year curriculum of golf course management will take courses in plant science, horticulture, and biology, as well as more traditional business, math, and English courses.

Other less rigorous programs are available for those unwilling or unable for now to commit to a four-year curriculum. Augusta Technical College, in Georgia, is one of several schools to provide a curriculum preparing graduates for employment both in the clubhouse and on the course. It lasts one year—four quarters—and includes courses in accounting, pest control, marketing, fundamentals of selling, turf management, and interpersonal relations. Employment opportunity leads are posted following graduation. View the complete curriculum on its web site (*http://augusta.tec.ga.us/academic/d_golf.htm*), to see if this is the kind of program that would interest you. If so, research schools offering similar programs in areas closer to you.

Another two-year program is at Sandhills Community College, in the Pinehurst, North Carolina, area. For more information about this program, including financial aid possibilities, the Sandhills web address is *www.sandhills.cc.n.c.us/turf/turfmain.html.* If a two-year program is a possibility for you, if not now, perhaps in a year or two, research those schools offering golf course management programs that are more convenient to you.

GOLF CAREER-RELATED WEB SITES

- **GolfCourse.com** (*www.golfcourse.com*)
  Search tool for accessing information on golf courses, resorts, and clubs. Includes a course locator and information on travel, architecture, and environment.

- **GolfWeb** (*www.golfweb.com*)
  Golf-related information, including a library of articles and references, tour information, and course information.

- **iGOLF** (*www.igolf.com*)
  Contains information on the world of golf, mostly about the people who play the game and those who follow them. Subjects range from tournaments and travel to equipment and instruction.

- **Shaw Guides: Golf Schools and Camps** (*www.shawguides.com/golf*)

Detailed descriptions of hundreds of golf schools, camps for junior golfers, career and college programs, publications, and organizations worldwide.

A FEW KEY POINTS TO REMEMBER

- If you enjoy working with others and have the ability to communicate clearly, retail sales positions are excellent entry-level jobs with considerable opportunity for advancement.
- Part-time positions during peak selling seasons are an ideal way of investigating retail positions to see where they may lead.
- What to learn from Daq: (1) If you are mechanically adept and learn quickly, working in a shop is a great career path for anyone getting out of high school. (2) If you are skilled, you can find an atmosphere to work in that suits you and allows you to work at something you care about.
- What to learn from Gunther: (1) If you know a game well—and also love and respect it—you can be a good official. (2) Officiating can be difficult, but this same knowledge, love, and respect for the game can keep you going. (3) Soccer is one of the sports in which there is a growing acceptance of girls and women as officials.

CHAPTER SIX

Self-Employment Career Opportunities

There are other sports and fitness employment opportunities in areas that may not have occurred to you. For the most part they don't offer the multiple-occupation potential you've seen in previous chapters, but they may tie in to other interests you have. For example, you may want to research one or more of the following, either on-line or in your local public library: smoke jumper, ski patroller, avalanche forecaster, underwater photographer, small-plane pilot, hurricane chaser, and U.S. Navy SEAL.

There is another characteristic that differentiates the following three professionals from those you've read about earlier in this book. Not all sports, fitness, and recreation careers require working according to an employer's rules and timetable, with paychecks never as large as they should be. You can always start your own business and keep a larger percentage of the revenues.

Then why do so few recent high school grads decide to work for themselves? Mostly because business start-ups take more seed money than they are likely to have. The businesses also take all of their spare time, and add to this the uneasiness they'll feel every step of the way with no idea what to expect next.

PHYSICAL FITNESS ENTREPRENEUR

For those of you who are undaunted and still want to know more about starting your own business, here are a few circumstances and qualities that you will find indispensable:

- You don't mind taking risks.

- You have a financial cushion that allows you to lose some money until your business begins to make money.

- You're good at what you do, and have identified a market for your services in the geographical area you have selected.

On the following pages are the stories of three people who work for themselves. All are highly motivated professionals All started their careers working for others, and when they thought the time was right, decided to strike out on their own. Other than this, they are quite different from one another, with quite different interests and career goals. They have also arrived at their current situations in very different ways. See for yourself—from their own words.

A Person Who's Done It

MEET PATRICK "SARGE" AVON

VITAL STATISTICS

After five years in the U.S. Navy, Patrick Avon was fired from two jobs that didn't interest him. Another employer went out of business, but that job did interest him. The company name was available for $500, so Patrick bought it. That was in 1989. Today Sarge Corp. is a multimillion-dollar workout business with offices in several cities, and Patrick has written a book version of his program called Boot Camp: Be All You Used to Be. *Here is the way it all happened:*

Boot camp was my favorite part of the Navy. I loved it. I was a dental technician, but my love was fitness. Not that the conditions were so great. Working out aboard ship is different from exercising in a gym. It takes a lot of patience to wait between the ship's rolls to do a bench press. We were on an aircraft carrier one deck below the jet landing area, cramped in a tiny room with F-14s landing 15 feet (5 m) above us every 90 seconds. There was no circulation, but did we complain? Heck no; at 18 years old we were more grateful than you can imagine to be saved from "Gilligan's Island" reruns, which was all our shipboard video library had to offer!

I never thought I could duplicate that experience. When I got out of the Navy and was working for a leasing company, I got a part-time fitness instructor's job at The Sergeant's Program, a military-style workout company in Rockville, Maryland. The fit was unbelievable; it was a perfect match. My style was much like it was when I was a physical training leader in Navy boot camp—a lot of yelling. Partly this was showmanship and partly it was motivational.

Then a bad winter came along, and most of the clients quit, and without clients I had no job. I still worked for the leasing company, but I was really getting bored with the routine. A couple of years later I had finally had enough. I went back to the owners of Sergeant's and asked if I could buy the company name. They said, "Sure," and I paid them $500. They had no trademark, no license, no brochure, no client list, so the name was essentially all there was to buy.

The first thing I did was to contact the five guys who were in the last class I taught. I told them I wanted to put this thing back together, and that I'd give a discount to each of them who showed up with another person who wanted to join. Then I got married, and scheduled the next session the day after I got back from my honeymoon. At the next session all five of them showed up, plus three new clients! The following session 16 people showed up—and I was on my way. I charged $50 a month, and after six months I was making more with "Sarge" part time than I was with the leasing company full time.

One of my clients was a printer and printed brochures and business cards for me as a favor. I put my posters up high enough on telephone poles so they couldn't be torn down easily, but after a few months the county got wise, and the sheriff told me if I didn't take them down, the city would fine me $50 per sign per day. I don't know if that was because of how high I had put them on the poles, or what the signs said ("I'M GOING TO GET YOUR BUTT IN SHAPE!"). In any case, this didn't go over too well in the affluent suburb of Chevy Chase—and the signs came down in a hurry!

At that point the word was already out on the street, because nobody had ever done anything like this. I started running with it and within a year I had picked up another 50 to 75 clients. I was teaching classes in the morning, putting up posters at night (until the sheriff stopped me), and hustling for more business on weekends, which didn't leave much time for the leasing company. I wasn't getting much sleep, but I was making great money!

After about a year the leasing company fired me, and I went into this thing full time. I mean, you can't blame them; I was driving around with the Sarge logo both on the door and the back of my Jeep Wrangler, and my vanity plate read "LOSE FAT." Roughly a year into the business I went full time.

My typical day now is very different from the way it used to be. It's still very business-oriented, but I lead leaders now. I still do customer service, a lot of interviews, a lot of community events. I troubleshoot relationships. For example if we have a customer who hasn't paid us in a long time, I'll call. We always get the money when I call—and I don't even need to go into the "Sarge mode."

One thing I always have time for is to teach my 6:00 A.M. class. We've gotten some attention over the past couple of years by holding early morning workouts in front of Dunkin' Donuts and McDonald's drive-throughs. We'll be doing pushups as the smell of fresh breakfast sandwiches and coffee floats over our heads. The customers get a kick out of it, and many of them stop to watch. When I have a small audience I'll yell at the class just to have some fun with the situation, something like: "Smell those doughnuts, people? Well, you're not getting any! They'll just make you fat, anyway."

As a corporation, we've grown a lot in the past ten years. Today, in our corporate headquarters I have a chief operating officer, a vice president of business operations, an office manager, a receptionist, three salespeople, and a head instructor. In our Chicago office is a head instructor and a general manager. We also have an office in Washington, D.C., and soon we'll open in Atlanta and Los Angeles.

We sponsor a lot of races in these cities, as well. We put on the 7-mile (11-km) "Jolly Fat Man's Run" every year, sponsored by the U.S. Marine Corps. All of the proceeds go to Toys for Tots. The race started with only four guys, and has grown to about 175 to 200. And these are people doing 7 miles, in decent time, who had never exercised! Then after a race we'll have a party and I'll speak to the 250 or so guests. I get a real charge out of that.

This is not all about the size of this operation, though. There's a woman in our program I always brag about because she went from a size 20 to a size 8.

Also, when I hear of somebody going off Prozac because she doesn't need it anymore, that makes me feel fantastic. Or if someone who had been taking diabetic medicine now doesn't need it because he got his weight down, that's a terrific feeling. This alone has made it all worthwhile. It's what I'll take with me when I hang it up in 30 years or so.

SPORTS PUBLIC RELATIONS SPECIALIST

Public relations specialists work as "promoters" for businesses, governments, universities, and hospitals. Their most important job is to build and maintain positive relationships with the public. In sports, fitness, and recreation organizations, public relations specialists promote the interests of professional, college, and corporate-sponsored sports teams; cruise lines and resorts; sports equipment retailers; and multi-club health corporations. (Public relations specialists working on behalf of The Sports Authority, Carnival Cruise Lines, the YMCA, and Bally's Total Fitness contributed information or names of key people that led to help with four of the chapters in this book.)

Opportunities in public relations are best for college graduates who combine a degree in journalism, advertising, or other communications-related fields. Entering public relations without a college degree is difficult, but not impossible. Those of you interested in a public relations career are advised to get assignments while you're in high school, even if you work as a volunteer, so you can point to experience an employer can help you build on, rather than try to enter the field cold, which will be next to impossible without a connection or personal contact. The name for such experience is "internship," and that's what you should call it on your résumé (see pages 10–11). The more early experience you can pile up, the easier it will be for you to leverage yourself into a career beyond high school, not just in public relations, by the way, but in any of the occupations covered in *Success Without College: Careers in Sports, Fitness, and Recreation*.

THE RIGHT STUFF

The ability to write and speak well is essential to success in public relations. Heather Parrish, a Chicago-area account executive says, "You have to have a big interest in reading and writing. English skills are the most important; math doesn't matter nearly as much. High school graduates with writing skills and boldness can work themselves into an entry-level job, but it's hard, and you can't give up. I sent my résumé to 60 or 70 agencies before I got a call back. When I got my first job it was like crossing the finish line.

"One of the biggest things kids can do for themselves is to learn how to write a press release. Just go to a company's web site on the Internet, go to their "News" or "Corporate Information" page, and you'll usually find that this is where they post their press releases. There you can get an idea of what is newsworthy, and what angles are important. Another good way to learn is through a software program. Microsoft Word has a good one. The next biggest thing to do is keep abreast of what is going on in the daily newspapers. Read as many as you can."

WHAT SPORTS PUBLIC RELATIONS SPECIALISTS DO

Patty Handscheigel, an account executive with several years experience in sports public relations, has assembled a list of the ten most important responsibilities of her job:

1. **Writing press releases.** This entails putting Who, What, Where, When, Why, and How into a written document for editors and reporters. You also have to create press kits, advisories, and other material, depending on the specific type of public relations.

2. **Media research.** Locating and contacting media editors, reporters, etc. This can be more of a task than you might think as you've got to be able to find information about the publication, and figure out which editor covers your type of story.

3. **Organizing and implementing your plan.** This is necessary for each person or event you work with. It includes setting a course of action: deciding who to contact, what to say, and when to say it.

4. **Providing assistance to media attending an event.** Making sure they have places to take photos or tape footage, providing information they may need, such as press releases and other information, arranging interviews with guests or participants, etc.

5. **Getting copies of everything that runs—either televised or in print.** This is your permanent record; it is essential in maintaining client relations, as well as getting new business. When you have several clients and many items running at the same time, this can be difficult—but be sure to stay with it.

6. **Assisting clients with interviewing skills.** Helping clients represent their company, school, or team effectively in public appearances is a part of your job; call it a transferable public relations skill.

7. **Finding angles within your story.** Not every reporter will automatically see the newsworthiness of your story. You must be creative, and customize your pitch to attract certain reporters—with statistics, or whatever it takes.

8. **Organizing media events and press tours.** An essential part of public relations is arranging meetings with newspaper writers and TV and radio reporters to convey information about a player or team.

9. **Following up on *everything*.** Be tenacious. Call back every reporter who has been sent information, to be sure he or she will be covering your story.

10. **Staying in touch with your sport or industry.** Read the trade magazines for your sport, as well as general publications such as *Sports Illustrated* and *Sport*, and the web sites for ESPN, Fox Sports, and Sports Illustrated/CNN, etc. It is important to be familiar with what the media is covering in sports, both from the business angle as well as from the fan's point of view.

WHAT THE JOB IS *REALLY* LIKE

"My days are really busy," says Heather Parrish. "I get to work early because New York media is an hour ahead of us; I need to hit *The New York Times* and *The Wall Street Journal* as early as possible. I try to be really respectful of the editors. I wish I knew more of them. From the time I get in at 8:30, it's instantly insane. I have about 50 or 60 e-mail messages to answer, then I work on my clients' press releases. I try to get all of my clients a place-ment a week. (A "placement" is a story—publicizing an agency client—that a public relations person is able to get newspapers and magazines to publish, or radio and TV stations to air.) This takes a lot of time on the phone, some days practically all of my time. Then on Fridays all of my reports are due."

A Person
Who's Done It

MEET HEATHER PARRISH

VITAL STATISTICS

Heather Parrish (not her real name) has followed a career path somewhat different from the norm, in that she was an athlete first, and then worked her way into public relations. Here is how she did it:

When I graduated from high school, I wanted to be a preschool teacher. While I was taking courses that would lead to the certificate I needed, I worked as a volunteer at a child-care center. After less than a year, I realized that the field was not for me.

I moved to Chicago from my hometown near the Wisconsin border, and after a few months of rollerblading, shopping, and hanging out with friends, I decided to pursue my first love: hockey. I found a number of friends as interested in starting a women's in-line hockey league as I was. Within a year we had formed the first women's in-line hockey league in Illinois. I was 21.

The hockey was great, but another aspect of the experience intrigued me even more. The league had hired a public relations consultant from a small, independent firm to publicize our league. She was sharp, she was professional, she wrote well, and she made some really great placements.

At first we spent a lot of time together because I was the main media contact for her. I was fascinated, and when she saw I was interested in what she did, she really took me under her wing, both by coaching and by example. She taught me to talk slowly and clearly. She taught me to put an interview in perspective, and to bring it back into focus when the interviewer strayed from the subject. She also taught me how to write a good press release. Eventually, I realized that I was able to do it, and could be really passionate about it. I wish I knew where she was today, so I could tell her what a great influence she was on my life. I've looked for her, but I've never been able to find her.

What I realized was that I could do it! I took every opportunity I could to write a press release, to get good coverage. Nobody paid me anything, but that was OK, because I knew that if I made the sacrifice and put my best foot forward, I had enough self-confidence to get that foot in the door. When we moved the team to Los Angeles, I had some great placements, including several on the 10:00 P.M. news sports segment on Fox.

People used to tell me there was no way I was ever going to get a women's hockey team on TV, but I did. I just called them. I always have a lot of energy talking about the clients I represent, and I guess it shows.

I also did PR for our Seattle team, and one back in rural Minnesota, both for hockey and for women's baseball. That's when I decided to get serious. I took about six months to get my life in order—I had just turned 25—and realized there were actual PR agencies one could work for. I didn't know much about the industry, just that I liked it.

Two and a half years ago I got my big break. I was up in Wisconsin and saw an ice arena that should have been doing well, but wasn't. I told the owner specifically what I thought I could do for him in terms of publicity, and he hired me—for $7 an hour! It was absurd, but it was a start. He started me out in group sales, and in six months I had made 35 placements. He raised me to $10.25, which is very good money for that area. This was a great opportunity for me, because I was free to do whatever I needed to, to get more business in there.

I built up enough experience so that I was able to move on to another, bigger agency, with more money. At this agency there are no sports clients, but that could change. If it doesn't, I'll just go back to doing it on my own again. Handling sports is what I like most to do. To do well in this business I know I need more education, which is why I'm taking courses at the University of Wisconsin.

Still, I don't know if there are many people out there who feel as good as I do about the way they make a living. I hope so. There's no better feeling than to call a marketing director and be able to say, "I have good news. You're going to be on CNBC," and then listen to them yell. If you can do something that gives you this kind of a charge in your life, go for it. I loved this business when I started in it, and I love it just as much now.

USEFUL WEB SITE

- **Women's Sports Foundation** (*www.womenssportsfoundation.org*) Comprehensive source for exploring careers in sports and fitness, including career placement services, job listings, and networking opportunities.

MASSAGE THERAPIST

"I have a college education—a master's degree, in fact," says Jan Tripp, a certified massage therapist with her own business in Gaithersburg, Maryland. "So in one sense I really don't qualify for this book. But at the same time, a college degree has nothing to do with qualifying to become a massage therapist."

THE RIGHT STUFF

Jan completed a 510-hour program at the Baltimore School of Massage. "In Maryland, you have to have a high school diploma to qualify for massage training," she says. "I think that before long at least 20 credits at a community college will be required as well. A lot of states are trying to upgrade their requirements, to cause the medical profession and the public to take us more seriously as healthcare professionals.

"In my class there were several adults who were changing careers, a few 20-somethings, and a couple of kids right out high school. I completed the professional training program, and then passed the National Certification Board for Therapeutic Massage and Bodywork. We took physiology, anatomy, and body mechanics, and went through the circulatory system, muscular system, skeletal system, and nervous system. We also learned how to set up a business.

"For recertification every four years we must have logged a minimum of 200 hours of work experience and 50 hours of continuing education credits. I document the hours for all of the people I work on. In the state of Maryland we need to be certified by the Board of Chiropractic. I also belong to the American Massage Therapy Association, the principal benefit of which is the liability insurance they provide."

WHAT THE JOB IS *REALLY* LIKE

"I work about six hours a week at the National Fitness Institute," says Jan. "The patients are those who have had recent back surgery or who have a recurring back problem. Two physical therapists are responsible for their rehabilitation, and I work on them as well. Usually on Fridays I work at a chiropractor's clinic. There are three of us who come in on different days. The nice part is that when the workload is light we can treat our own clients there.

"On weekends I usually work at the Fleet Feet Running Store. This is a serious running store that carries only running equipment. When customers come in we watch them run, analyze their stride, find out what their needs are, and help them find shoes that will give them the support they need. I get referrals from them—also a pretty good equipment discount.

"But my favorite place to work is here, in my home. It's where I do most of my business."

A Person Who's Done It

MEET JAN TRIPP

VITAL STATISTICS

Massage therapy is Jan Tripp's fifth career. After earning a degree in education, Jan's first job was as a Poet-in-the-Schools for grades one through six. Next she worked at IBM for seven years. Jan then apprenticed to a blacksmith and worked at a forge for 14 years. Career number four was running competitively, as well as acting as a volunteer running coach, which is where she got the idea to get into her current profession.

Most of my success has come from having my own business, but you really have to be out there hustling to make a go of it—that and making good contacts.

One good thing about massage therapy is that there are so many areas you can get into. You can work in a spa, go into some of the healing therapies, pregnancy massage, sports massage . . . the opportunities are endless. I know that most people who go through the school hope to make a career of it, but there are others who use massage therapy as a way of supporting themselves if they decide to go back to college.

What makes me love this profession is the change that comes over people after they've been here three or four times. At about that time you can see them beginning to take charge of their own health. They start to realize how much control they have over how they feel and who they are. In this sense we try to help people help themselves, rather than take the responsibility of curing them.

Sometimes they come here in incredible pain, then when they start to feel better, they begin to pay attention to what their bodies are telling them. They start to wonder *why* they hurt in a particular place.

You can sense the emergence of this sense of empowerment, which in a way parallels the physical benefits of massage. It's the client beginning to say, "I'm worth taking care of myself." And it's just a wonderful thing to see.

USEFUL WEB SITES

- **Baltimore School of Massage** (*www.bsom.com*)
  You may not live close enough to Baltimore to attend this school, but by going through the site you'll get a good idea of what is involved in completing a comprehensive massage therapy program. Other areas covered: frequently asked questions, continuing education, descriptions of various programs offered, and links to additional information.

- **American Massage Therapy Association** (*www.amtamassage.org*)
  Professional organization for 42,000 member massage therapists in 30 countries. Information on accreditation, AMTA events, job network, and information exchange message center.

- **Bancroft School of Massage Therapy** (*http://www.bancroftmt.com*)
  Information on muscular pain relief, educational and continuing educational programs, and the schools history, alumni, and faculty.

- **Massage Therapy Schools Q&A** (*www.naturalhealers.com*)
  This site provides a directory of schools. Individuals interested in pursuing a career in massage therapy can read answers to some of the most commonly asked questions about the profession.

- **Massage Therapy Network** (*www.massagetherapy.net*)
  This site provides a directory of massage schools, clinics, and therapists by state.

- **Massage Therapy.com** (*www.massagetherapy.com*)
  This site provides a directory of legitimate, professional therapists, schools, and products.

- **Seattle Massage School** (*www.seattlemassageschool.com*)
  This site provides valuable information for would-be masseuses.

- **Virginia School of Massage** (*www.vasom.com*)
  This site provides information about the school's professional 100-hour basic program, and 500-hour massage therapy program.

A FEW KEY POINTS TO REMEMBER

• People considering self-employment should (1) not mind taking risks; (2) have a source of income until the business begins to make money; (3) be good at what they do, and have a market for it.

• What to learn from Patrick: To start your own business and make it thrive takes a lot of hard work and the willingness to take chances.

• What to learn from Heather: If you know what you want to do but aren't successful at first, keep trying. (See the list of the ten most important public relations responsibilities on pages 93–95.)

• What to learn from Jan: The goal is to help people help themselves, not simply cure them.

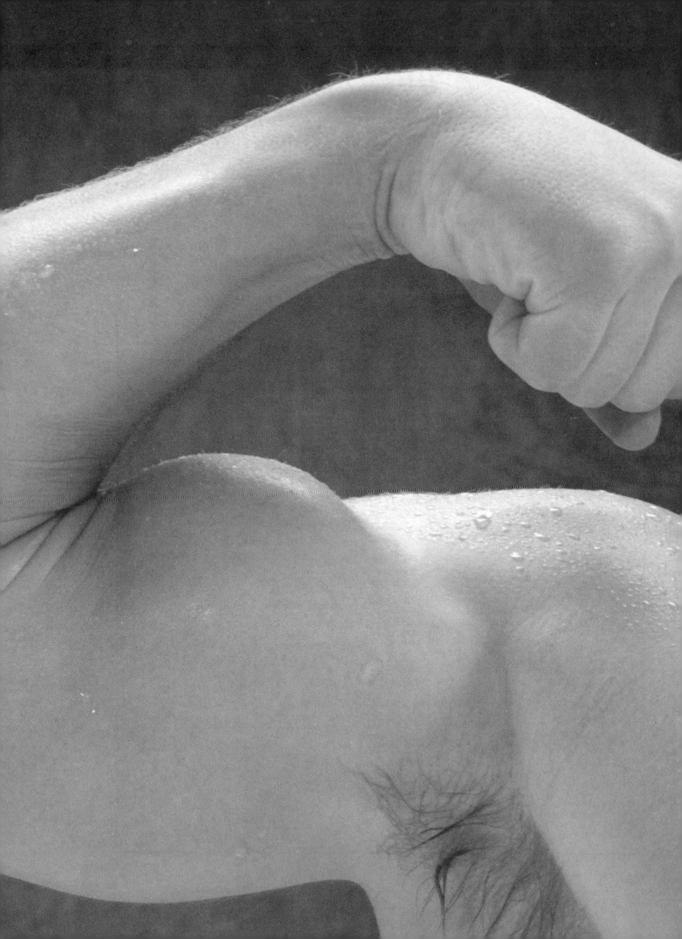

CHAPTER SEVEN

Creating Powerful Résumés and Cover Letters

The résumé is a multipurpose tool, critical to your job search. A good résumé should

- tell employers you are available

- reflect parts of your personality through its content and style

- display your job-related accomplishments, skills, responsibilities, and highlights.

Another purpose a résumé has is to represent your job-related strengths as clearly and as powerfully as possible. If this is done effectively, the job-related accomplishments and skills you have will make you look like a better candidate than you thought you were. The result: Your self-confidence will go up, and you'll perform better in every aspect of your job search.

With all of these responsibilities, a résumé must be put together with particular care. All of its pieces must interlock in such a way that each flows smoothly to the next. To reach this level of quality, be prepared to write several drafts, deleting phrases and words that are irrelevant or repetitious, adding others as they're needed, and constantly reworking each entry until you're satisfied that it is as good as it can possibly be.

One reason for all of this attention to detail is that a résumé must communicate both totally and instantly. Many employers say that within 15 to 20 seconds they can tell whether to save a résumé for further consideration or throw it out. Whether you learn about a job opening from a classified ad or from the Internet, there may be dozens of other candidates. With this volume of response, company résumé readers find themselves reading to *exclude* candidates rather than *include* them.

For example, the director of human resources in a large ski resort needs to hire a new instructor. She specifies five essential skills or kinds of experience she wants her readers in the department to look for in an applicant. If those qualities don't appear prominently in the résumé, out goes the résumé. In such situations, 10 to 20 seconds may be as much time as an applicant has to make the first cut.

This means the various elements that a potential employer is looking for—dependability, ambition, ability to work with people—must pop out and catch the reader's eye. You can accomplish this by placement, and the creative use of type and "white space." By <u>underlining</u>, or using **boldface** or *italics*, or putting certain words or phrases in CAPITAL LETTERS—all done in a consistent, systematic way—different elements of a résumé can be made more visible. Similarly, by putting some "air" between entries (spacing some kinds of data horizontally or vertically from others), all of the elements can be made easier to read, and more data can be taken in at a single reading; for example, two- to four-line entries are far easier to read than dense paragraphs of eight to ten lines, and are therefore far more likely to *get* read (see pages 120–125).

ORGANIZING YOUR RÉSUMÉ

There are dozens of ways résumés can be written. If you check your local bookstore you'll find ten or more experts giving contradictory advice on the humble act of résumé preparation. Some writers, in fact, advise not using résumés at all. The advice we offer is based on a survey of sports and fitness directors and human resource professionals. In other words, we interviewed the interviewers to find out what specific qualities influenced their decision to keep a résumé or throw it out. Here is a summary of the survey results, broken down according to Content, Clarity, and Style.

CONTENT

- Be sure the reader of your résumé can identify both your immediate objective and a summary of your job-related qualifications.

- Describe your accomplishments for part-time and summer jobs using specific numbers where they are appropriate, as well as your specific duties for each job.

- Emphasize accomplishments, skills, and responsibilities directly related to the job you are seeking.

- Always include career-related volunteer experience.

CLARITY

- For easier reading, limit job and accomplishment descriptions to four lines. (Longer descriptions usually can be divided into two parts.)

- Double-check to eliminate errors or inconsistencies in grammar or punctuation.

- Always ask at least one other person whose language skills you respect to read it—your English teacher, for example.

- Be sure to clearly label all personal data: name, address, phone, e-mail, and fax numbers.

- Record your job history in reverse chronological order.

APPEARANCE

- Invest in a quality printing job.

- Choose paper of good weight and quality, standard size, and conservative color (white, gray, or off-white.)

- Avoid attention-getting special effects, for example, the inclusion of artwork or photographs, bizarre type styles, or a brochure format.

- Try to limit your résumé to one page, but use a second page for overflow rather than crowding essential copy.

- Take all measures necessary to eliminate typographical errors, even if you have to pay an expert.

TARGETING

Good writers write for specific audiences. For résumé writers, this means writing to address your readers' specific needs. To do this you have to communicate three essential levels of information:

1. a knowledge of your specialty
2. a knowledge of your prospective employer
3. a knowledge of the position available

The way you describe your education is crucial. Do your best to emphasize how comprehensive and relevant what you have learned is to the opportunity you are seeking. Also, include any summer, part-time, or volunteer jobs you have held, giving the most space and attention to those in the sports, fitness, and recreation industries, where applicable. Putting together the best possible résumé requires that you assemble all the professional, personal, and educational data that are relevant. This brings us to the components of the résumé itself.

RÉSUMÉ COMPONENTS

OBJECTIVE

After identifying yourself by name, address, phone and fax numbers, and e-mail address, tell the reader what specific job you want. This Objective, along with the Summary section that follows it, sets the tone and positioning for the entire résumé. These two sections will provide a framework and perspective for every word that follows.

In most instances, your objective will mirror the occupation you have chosen; for example:

OBJECTIVE: Kayak Instructor

OBJECTIVE: Bicycle Mechanic

OBJECTIVE: Personal Trainer

OBJECTIVE: Fishing Guide

If you have a strong preference for circumstances beyond the job itself—for instance, where you want to work—this is where to put it. Example:

OBJECTIVE: Massage Therapist on a Cruise Ship

You'll probably want to prepare two versions of your résumé to accommodate your setting preference. This way you can use the more specialized version for all of the fitness centers or health clubs within your geographical area, and if that doesn't work switch to the generic version (OBJECTIVE: Massage Therapist) for the remaining opportunities. Through this strategy you'll let cruise line human resource directors know that you'd be most comfortable in that setting, the implication being that you'd do your best work there. And in non-cruise ship situations you can use a version of your résumé that doesn't mention your preference, and therefore doesn't work against you—a minor distinction, perhaps, but one that might be effective enough to give you the edge you need.

SUMMARY

While the Objective tells the reader exactly what you want to do, the Summary section tells in very specific terms why you are qualified to do it. The Summary should distill your background down to two or three sentences that emphasize your skills, accomplishments, and any special qualifications you may have for the Objective written just above it. Here is one written by a SCUBA instructor:

> SUMMARY: Fifteen years SCUBA diving experience, progressing through YMCA leadership program to become an instructor, specialty instructor, and instructor trainer. Diving experience includes Lake Champlain, New York; North Carolina shipwrecks; Florida Keys; Cozumel, Mexico; Hawaii; and Alaska. Coordinated and conducted annual YMCA SCUBA convention in 1995.

Every word in this Summary is position-specific, intended to match the applicant's credentials with the responsibilities of the job. The sole purpose of this careful matching is to improve the odds for a job interview. The Summary is your best advance sales tool, so make the most of it.

WRITING YOUR SUMMARY

The Objective states what job you're after. The Summary tells why you're qualified to do it. Complete the following form to help you write your Summary. In terms of the type of position you are seeking, what significant accomplishments highlighted your part-time and summer jobs? Any high school awards? Above-average grades? A vocational curriculum in the occupation you are seeking? If so, these should be mentioned, and explained in detail later in the résumé.

POSITION #1 (MOST RECENT):
Title: _____

OVERALL DUTIES AND RESPONSIBILITIES:
1. _____
2. _____
3. _____
4. _____

SIGNIFICANT ACHIEVEMENTS:

What was the problem? _____

_____

What did you do about it? _____

_____

_____

What were the results? (quantify if possible) _____

_____

_____

What abilities or skills were required? _____

_____

_____

(Repeat for other volunteer, summer, and part-time jobs.)

Now go back and circle those duties, accomplishments, and abilities that relate most closely to the position listed in your Objective. Try to make the best fit possible between the job you want and your qualifications. Use only those accomplishments that relate specifically to the position you are seeking.

Using your circled items, write on a separate sheet of paper the summary of your qualifications for the position. (Refer to the sample résumés on pages 120–125 for models.) For maximum effectiveness, your Summary should be no longer than three or four sentences.

Look at what you've written:

- Is it clear?

- Is it interesting?

- Are the ideas linked logically?

Write as many additional drafts as necessary to be satisfied with the result.

THE EXPERIENCE SECTION

Men and women in their twenties and thirties, veterans of several years in the working world, have an opportunity to write résumés that include impressive, hard-earned responsibilities and accomplishments. This gives potential employers a much clearer picture of the way these applicants will perform on the job.

Fresh from high school with no permanent, full-time job experience, you obviously don't have this luxury, but you do have assets; not least among them is the fact that an employer won't be expecting an accomplishments-loaded résumé. Go back to your Summary worksheet on pages 110–111. Treat all of your volunteer work and summer and part-time jobs as though they were your livelihood. Write up the most recent position first, with as much career-related detail as you can think of.

Remember that your résumé will be important in your interview. Accomplishments should be broken up into bite-sized, one-sentence pieces, allowing the interviewer to locate and absorb them quickly. You as the interviewee should view each entry as the basis for a leading question, for which you have rehearsed responses that will allow you to answer in ten seconds, if asked, or to go on for several minutes, depending on how interested the interviewer is.

Think of your résumé as a script, both for you and the interviewer. This is particularly true of the experience section. Each entry is a cue to be picked up by the interviewer as appropriate, and singled out for further questions, especially if it relates to the position available.

Using a similar style, go back to the Summary worksheet that includes your job-by-job duties and accomplishments, and put them in final form for your experience section. (Look also at the sample résumés on pages 120–125 as models.) In writing and laying out this section, remember to make all entries as clear and as visible as possible, allowing your reader to take in your strengths at a single glance, and select for more careful reading those that relate closely to the target position. The layout of your résumé, in fact, is as important as its content.

MISCELLANEOUS PERSONAL ENTRIES

Opinion varies as to whether to include some of the following frequently seen résumé entries. Here are ours:

- Career-related hobbies?   **Yes.**

- Height, weight, marital status?   **No.**

- State of health?   **No** (It's always "excellent" anyway).

- Include a photograph?   **No.**

- "References available on request"?   **No** (When they're needed, you'll be asked).

PUTTING YOUR RÉSUMÉ TOGETHER

Using your completed worksheets, and referring to the samples on pages 120–125, write the first draft of your résumé on a separate piece of paper. Try to get the essential information on no more than one printed page, but if your background justifies it, don't worry if the final version goes onto a second page. Hint: When writing your résumé, always keep your objective in mind.

- Write as many drafts as necessary to produce a finished product that pleases you.

- Ask family members, friends, and, if possible, someone from your career group to read your final draft and suggest additions, cuts, or changes.

- Have your résumé word processed and printed by a professional, unless you have exceptional skills in these areas.

RÉSUMÉS FOR THE INTERNET

Those of you using Internet sources as part of your job search (see Chapter Eight, pages 133–136) will need to prepare a completely different version of your résumé. Forget about paper quality, type size and face, and some of the other visual elements covered earlier in this chapter. Many electronic job-search services have their own fill-in-the-blanks form; others offer more leeway regarding space. In either case, the burden of communication will be borne largely by the words you use.

In essence, the on-line and Internet job-search services act as your electronic personnel agency, except that *you* do more of the work. There is another similarity that works to your advantage. The physical appearance of a résumé is less important to a client working through an employment agency than, for example, an employer you apply to directly. This means that the pressure is off regarding paper and type decisions. These will be made for you.

The control you do have over appearance has to do largely with spacing: Use white space to set you apart from the other type-dense résumés downloaded by employers.

Keywords

Most employers and employment agencies who use the Internet to find prospective candidates simplify their searches by the use of "keywords"—nouns or phrases that describe a candidate's specific skills or area of expertise. Electronic scanners pick up these keywords from the résumés of potential candidates as a means of identifying individuals meriting further consideration.

WRITING A BASIC COVER LETTER

You are one of several job candidates who seem to be equal in most areas. What do you do to improve your chances of getting an interview? What do job candidates of seemingly equal worth do to stand the best chance of getting an interview? Without full-time experience, after all, recent high school graduates applying for the same job can look very much alike on paper.

A well-written cover letter gives you an opportunity to introduce yourself to prospective employers in "human" terms, as your résumé cannot. The qualities most employers are looking for in an entry-level staff member are enthusiasm, dedication, loyalty, the ability to be a "team player," and others you'll see listed in the ad describing the position. All of these can be demonstrated, either implicitly or explicitly, in your cover letter.

You'll need a basic cover letter format you can adapt for each of the situations that require a mailed résumé. Letters for any purpose should never look as though they have been mass-produced. If they do, it will virtually guarantee that your résumé will see the bottom of a wastebasket rather than getting read.

Here are the situations for which you'll want to develop cover letters:

- Responses to newspaper or trade magazine ads

- Introductions to employment agencies

- Applications to specific employers

The sample letter on page 119 is an application to a specific employer. Like any good cover letter, regardless of the situation, it contains four elements:

1. **Attention.** Grab your reader immediately, to be sure the rest of the letter gets read. This needn't be cute or gimmicky. If you are answering an ad, just state your business in a straightforward way, mentioning the position being advertised, when and where it was advertised, and your interest in filling it. If you are applying for a job without knowing whether an opening exists, one way to start is to mention something about the company, store, or facility to which you are writing. Rely on a recent news story if you can—a new development that you read about recently, such as a change of presidents, maybe, or the announcement of a new product or division, that may have triggered your letter in the first place.

2. **Interest.** In this section you'll need to describe in hard-hitting fashion the qualities you believe will get the reader's attention. These qualities should answer the need referred to in the attention paragraph. If you are answering an ad, all of the job requirements mentioned should be dealt with *in the exact order in which they were listed*. If five requirements were specified, you should be able to respond positively to the first three, or three of the first four, to expect an interview invitation. Deal only with requirements you can fill. Don't mention the ones you can't.

3. **Conviction.** Substantiate with one or two accomplishments your ability to do the job you are applying for. Build your case in terms as strong as you can make them.

4. **Action.** A good cover letter needs to move the reader to action. In the sample letter on page 119, you'll notice that the writer requests an interview. By indicating that you intend to call in person for an interview, you increase your chances of getting it. There's some psychological warfare at work here: A reader who knows a call is coming will feel compelled to deal with the matter in some way, if only to fend off the caller. (The downside: The person you're trying to reach may simply tell a secretary or assistant not to put your call through.) By making the call in the first place, however, you reduce the possibility of your letter not being dealt with.

Below is a worksheet to help you plot the four elements of a master cover letter that you can adapt for individual situations:

1. **Attention.** Write and refine two or three ways you might capture the reader's attention.
   Hint: Refer to a prospective employer's need.

   a. _____
   _____

b. _____

_____

c. _____

_____

2. **Interest.** Write and refine two or three ways to answer the question, "Why should the employer be interested in me?"
   Hint: Emphasize your strong points. Show how your qualities can fulfill the employer's need.

a. _____

_____

b. _____

_____

c. _____

_____

3. **Action.** Choose one or two accomplishments that demonstrate the strength of your experience.
   Hint: You'll need to change these for each letter you send, to make them fit the respective situation as closely as possible.

a. _____

_____

b. _____

_____

c. _____

_____

4. **Action.** Write and refine your closing paragraph.
   Hint: Don't leave it up to the prospective employer to call you.

Having done your homework, you are now ready to respond effectively to employment opportunities.

SAMPLE SPORTS, FITNESS, AND RECREATION RÉSUMÉS AND COVER LETTER

The résumés and cover letter on the following pages were written by several of the sport, fitness, and recreation professionals whose stories appear in this book. Not all of them represent the best possible examples of well-worded Summaries, Objectives, or job descriptions. (The subjects of the résumés, of course, did not have this book to consult when they wrote them!) They have been included primarily to illustrate the career paths of these successful professionals—who started as you did, and some of whom continued their education as they gained additional experience in their specialties.

(Networking Job Lead Follow-up)

11869 Washington Place, Apt. C
Los Angeles, CA 90066
October 14, 2001

Mr. Allan Ruggerio
General Manager
Del Sol Health and Fitness Studio
2618 Rolando Boulevard
Watsonville, CA 95076

Dear Mr. Ruggerio:

Recently I learned from Dick Masterson, a friend who worked for you at Del Sol Health and Fitness Studio from 1999 until late last year, that you intend to expand your Studio training facilities effective January 1, 2002. I am relocating to the Santa Cruz area at about that time, and would like very much to be considered as a personal trainer when you determine your needs in this area.

As you will see from the enclosed résumé, I am an ACE-accredited personal trainer, having completed both their 40-hour and 60-hour programs. I am comfortable either in a large training and fitness environment or working with individual clients in their homes. I also have completed a series of six IDEA courses, including the effective use of cardiovascular equipment and power dumbbell training.

I am totally committed to a client-centered criteria. In other words, I believe in emphasizing safety-first, results-oriented, time-conscious (within the client's time schedule), and habit-forming training.

I look forward to hearing more about the direction your new expansion is taking, and to speaking with you about the possibility of joining your personal training staff. If I don't hear from you by November 15, I'll call to see if there is a good time to schedule an interview.

Sincerely,

Charles J. Larson
Enclosure: Résumé

CHARLES J. LARSON
11869 Washington Place, Apt C
Los Angeles, CA 90066
(310) 397-3525-home
(310) 775-5704-pager

OBJECTIVE

Seeking a position as a personal trainer, with a stable company, that offers me the opportunity to use my existing talents while continuing to develop new skills.

EDUCATION
April 2000

IDEA Personal Training Summit, West Anaheim, CA
15 hours of classes including (Functional Training Progressions), effective use of cardiovascular equipment, power dumbbell training and others.

April 1997

Progressive Fitness, Los Angeles, CA
Forty hour completion of an A.C.E. accredited program. Comprehensive review of theory, personal training and practical training.

November 1997

Progressive Fitness, Long Beach, CA
Sixty hour completion of an A.C.E. accredited program. This internship encompassed the practical and theoretical instruction in the art and science of closed-end training including: **Body Composition Analysis, Maximum Oxygen Uptake (VO$_2$ Max), Kinesiology, Strength Testing, Flexibility Testing, Trainer Assisted Stretching.**

EXPERIENCE
May 1998 to
December 1999

Bally Total Fitness
W. Los Angeles, CA
Customer service; counsel to establish specific health and fitness goals, determine individual fitness plans, continual body composition analysis, supervise individual workout sessions. Perform orientation workouts, assist club members with proper technique with machines and free-weights, enforcement of club rules and regulations, assist with training package sales and nutritional sales.

December 1999 to
Present

Independent Personal Training

**ACCREDITATIONS
AND
LICENSES**

American Council on Exercise
Personal Trainer, Certification No. T42880

REFERENCES

Available upon request

Robert D. Campbell
5865 N. 39th Street
Augusta, MI 49012

Phone 616.731.3088
Fax 616.731.3020
E-mail robertc@ymcasl.org

Objective   YMCA Executive Camp Director

Summary of   Thirteen years experience supervising YMCA camping activities; six
qualifications   years of additional camp counseling experience working with
junior and senior high school youth, as well as families. Excellent
teambuilder, program developer, and leader; supervisor of as many
as 90 staff members. Administer combined budgets in excess of $1
million. Totally committed to Y principles.

Work experience   Feb '99 to Present Sherman Lake YMCA Outdoor Center Augusta, MI
Director of Camping Services (Jan '00 to Present)

- Supervise year-round operations in Resident Camp, Day Camp,
  and Integrated Education School Programs; Summer Youth Camp
  programs for 3,500 6–16 year olds each summer; Spring, Fall,
  and Winter Integrated Educational School Programs for more
  than 4,000 students.

- Supervise three full-time and two part-time staff. Recruit, hire,
  and supervise 90 summer camp staff, including 3–4 international
  staff.

- Budget responsibility: $430,000 Resident Camp; $397,000 Day
  Camp; $271,000 Integrated Education School.

Resident Camp Director (Feb '99 to Dec '99)

- Created, developed, and directed first ever Summer Resident
  Camp at Sherman Lake Y for 570 6–16-year-old campers (which
  increased by 70 percent to 966 in 2000).

- Directed and facilitated Adventure Challenge Ropes
  Course/Climbing programs for school groups, corporate groups,
  and not-for-profit groups; recruited, hired, and supervised 35
  summer camp staff.

Dec '92 to Jan '99   Camp Nan A Bo Sho YMCA   Appleton, WI
Resident Camp Director

- Supervised year-round operations, including Summer Youth programs for 6–16-year-olds; Family Camp Weeks, and Parent/Child
  Weekends.

- Supervised two full-time staff. Recruited, hired, trained, and
  supervised 30 summer camp staff. Administered budget of
  $265,000.

- Facilitated 11.3% annual increase in camper enrollment for eight years

Aug '87 to Dec '92   Oshkosh Community YMCA   Oshkosh, WI
Day Camp Director/Youth Program Director

- Directed summer day camp operations, youth sports, and teen programs and special interest programs.

- Implemented a Counselor-in-Training program for potential camp leaders, with more than 50 youth participating.

- Increased football program enrollment from 49 to 140 over five years; with Oshkosh school system, developed city-wide youth basketball program for grades three through nine, with more than 200 participants.

Other Work Experience	Oct '85 to Jul '87—Omni Glass & Paint: Glazier; Architectural Technician
	Jun '84 to May '85—Oshkosh YMCA: Building Supervisor; Svc. Ctr. Attendant
	1978 to 1984 (when not in school or camp counseling)—UPS, Oshkosh Northwestern Newspaper, and carpentry work.
Education	1996–'97 Marion College, Appleton, WI $1\frac{1}{2}$ Semesters Bus. Admin.
	1980–'82; 1992 University of Wisconsin, Oshkosh $2\frac{1}{2}$ years music, general, and human service work
	1984–'85 Fox Valley Technical College, Oshkosh, WI Associate's Degree—Wood Technics
Community activities	Youth-Go (youth organization) award, 1995; church council member, worship and music committee, usher, counselor, and music director. National Exchange Club Director of the Year award, 1991. Oshkosh Coalition member and secretary. Oshkosh Young Life counselor and music leader.
YMCA Activities and Awards	YMCA of the USA Program Excellence Award for Camping, 1995–2000; Wisconsin MRC Program Excellence Award for Camping, 1995–1998; Michigan MRC Program Excellence Award for Camping, 1999–2000; APD (YMCA professional society) member since 1987; Wisconsin APD cabinet member, secretary, and newsletter editor, 1987–1996; APD Rookie of the Year, 1989; Wisconsin MRC youth sports coordinator and day camp coordinator, 1987–1992.
Interests and activities	Family time, singing, song writing, guitar, recording, photography, reading, camping, backpacking, climbing, fitness, and sports.

BETH DALZELL

SUMMARY
Fifteen years SCUBA diving experience, progressing through YMCA leadership program to instructor, specialty instructor, and instructor trainer, respectively. Diving experience includes Lake Champlain, New York, North Carolina shipwrecks; Florida Keys; Cozumel, Mexico; Hawaii, and Alaska. Coordinated and conducted annual YMCA SCUBA convention in 1985.

SCUBA EDUCATION
YMCA SCUBA Instructor Trainer
YMCA SCUBA Gold Instructor
- SLAM Instructor
- Wreck Diving Instructor
- Drysuit Instructor
International Association of Nitrox Divers
Divers Alert Network Oxygen Provider Instructor

RELATED EXPERIENCE
YMCA SCUBA and Snorkeling Instructor
- Montclair YMCA, Montclair, NJ
- Montclair YMCA Day Camp, West Milford, NJ

ADDITIONAL CERTIFICATIONS
CMAS SCUBA Instructor
National YMCA Certified Lifeguard
Red Cross CPR and First Aid Provider
D.A.N. O Provider
Certified NJ Teacher of the Handicapped, with Advanced Standing

AWARDS AND ACTIVITIES
Third Prize, Amateur Video Category, Beneath the Sea Dive Symposium
Head Coach, Columbia High School Swim Club, Maplewood, NJ

48 WOODSIDE TERRACE · EAST ORANGE, NEW YORK · 07052
PHONE 973.123.4567 · FAX 973.765.4321 · E-MAIL BETHNWES@YAHOO.COM

Jan G. Tripp
Certified Massage Therapist
Gaithersburg, MD
jthoofer@aol.com

THERAPEUTIC MASSAGE EDUCATION & PROFESSIONAL EXPERIENCE
Education: 500-hour Professional Massage Training Certificate, Baltimore School of Massage, MD. Curriculum included intensive hands-on instruction in Swedish, Deep Tissue, and Myofascial modalities; physiology and anatomy, clinical evaluation and correction approaches, introductions to reflexology and sports massage; client-practitioner relationship, ethics, holistic approaches to healing, and working in the school's public massage clinic.

Advanced courses in Myofascial Therapy for the Upper Extremities, Reiki, Stretching for Athletes, RRCA Coaching Certification, NeuroMuscular Therapy 1 (Posterior Spinal Muscles) & 3 (Lower Extremity), Orthopedic Massage Assessment, MotherMassage.

Nationally certified (282881-00) by the National Certification Board for Therapeutic Massage and Bodywork. State certified (M00332) by Maryland Board of Chiropractic Examiners.

Professional Experience:
1999 to present:
  – *Jan G. Tripp, Point-to-Point Therapeutic Massage*, Gaithersburg, MD: sole proprietor. Operate private massage therapy business within home and chiropractic office.

1999–2000:
  – *National Fitness Institute*, Rockville, MD: part-time massage therapist at fitness/spinal rehabilitation center. All type of clients; primarily deep tissue, NMT, and myofascial release massage, determined by brief clinical interview and assessment.
  – *Baltimore School of Massage*, Baltimore, MD: part-time teaching assistant for full-time therapeutic massage program. Assist in classroom and with students in deep tissue and myofascial bodywork.

Summer 2000:
  – *USA Track & Field Olympic Trials*, CA: massage therapist for Washington, DC-based track and field team.

Summer 1999:
  – *1999 AIDS Ride #4*, Raleigh, NC to Washington, DC: part of a team of massage therapists for 1700 riders and 500 crewmembers during the four-day ride.

OTHER WORK EXPERIENCE AND RELATED ACTIVITIES
1986 to 1999:
  – *Jan G. Tripp, Horseshoeing and Trimming*, Gaithersburg, MD: farrier. Created and operated, as sole proprietor, successful, full-time horseshoeing business in Montgomery County, MD.

1978 to 1984:
  – *IBM*, Rochester, MN and Yorktown Heights, NY: education & communications instructor and managing editor for in-house employee magazine.

1997 to present (volunteer):
  – *Montgomery Country Road Runners Club*, MD: running coach. Develop and lead running programs for beginning and intermediate runners.

OTHER EDUCATION
  MA in Education, 1978, Dept of Education, University of Minnesota, Minneapolis.

A FEW KEY POINTS TO REMEMBER

- A résumé must communicate both totally and instantly.
- Writing the best possible résumé requires assembling all of the professional, personal, and educational data relevant to an employer's specific needs.
- A well-written cover letter offers an opportunity to demonstrate enthusiasm, dedication, and an ability to work as a team player.

CHAPTER EIGHT

Marketing Yourself into a Good Job

Back in Chapter One we talked a bit about the many new sports, fitness, and recreation jobs that would become available between now and the next several years. Seven chapters later, this has not changed. But you mustn't think that because such jobs are being created at twice the pace of the economy as a whole they necessarily will be easy to land; in fact, the job market in these fields is more competitive today than it ever has been. This means that job seekers who depend *only* on the Yellow Pages, want ads, and employment agencies to generate leads are missing out on more than half the marketplace.

As a job seeker today, you need an edge. Often it's you against a sizable number of candidates who want the job you're after just as much as you do. Both timing and approach can be critical. There are ways other than through newspaper ads and agencies that can help spread the word that you exist and are available, and in some cases even allow you to be the first to apply for a job.

Not that you should avoid these two traditional sources; just don't depend on them exclusively, as so many others do. The most successful job seekers don't wait for the opportunities to come to them—they create their own opportunities.

How? By being as aware as possible of the market for their skills and specialty, whether they're looking in just the local metropolitan area, or in another nearby city where the jobs may be. On the following pages we'll not only show you how to get the most out of agencies and classified ads, but we'll also describe several other marketing strategies that likely will be even more effective in your search.

Traditional job-search sources for most high school grads:

• Telephone Book Yellow Pages

• Newspaper Want Ads

• Employment Agencies

Additional sources of possible use to career changers:

• Trade Publication Articles and Classifieds

• Database Services

• Professional Networks

• Internet Job Banks and Job Seeker Sites

YELLOW PAGES

The most obvious local source for job leads is your telephone book Yellow Pages. Just keep in mind that your future employer may not list its products or services in what you think is the most appropriate place. Yellow Page listings are not standardized, and vary from one location to another. So if you're looking for "Fitness Clubs" and find no listing, try "Health Clubs and Gymnasiums" or "Health and Fitness Program Consultants." If you can't find "SCUBA Instruction," look under "Dive Centers." In other words, don't give up if your specialty isn't where you expect it to be.

Let's say you're interested in working in a bicycle shop. Start under "Bicycles—Retail" or whatever your Yellow Pages publisher calls this category. This will acquaint you with all of the bicycle stores in the area. In a nearby city of 50,000 or more there should be a dozen such outlets. If you'd like to become a Tae Kwon Do or Karate instructor, look under "Martial Arts Instruction."

What you want to find out after putting together a list of likely sources of information—or with luck, a prospective employer—is whether there are jobs in your specialty you can commute to from home, or whether you'll have to move to another area for employment.

CALLS

In each call that you make to these sources, state your name and your purpose as simply and directly as you can. Work out the wording before you call and refer to your notes until you are comfortable working without them. A call may go something like this after you dial the number:

"Good morning, Kojo Academy of Tae Kwon Do. May I help you?"

"Yes, thank you. This is Gordon Cummings. I just graduated from Morris Hills Regional High School and am interested in becoming a Tae Kwon Do instructor. . . ."

"I'm sorry. We have no openings here."

"Yes, ma'am. I didn't think you did. My question is, is there someone in your office who might have heard of any opportunities in the area, either now or possibly within the next several months?"

At this point you could be completely blown off or, with luck, be turned over to someone who might have useful information for you. Just realize that there are a lot of opportunities out there for information, so try not to be discouraged if the first 10 or 15 calls end in rejection.

In the larger self-defense centers or health and fitness clubs, your introductory call will most likely be answered by a switchboard operator. In the smaller installations you'll probably speak first to an administrative assistant, or perhaps to one of the principals themselves. This is an important distinction for you because in the first instance an operator doesn't want to hear about your problem, only how to direct your call, by name or title. So, when calling a larger operation, ask first if the center has a human resources department. Because these people deal with employment, you might find someone willing to be helpful. A question that might get results, after you learn that no openings exist there, is: "Do you know of anybody in the area who is hiring fitness trainers, or who might be hiring them soon?"

If there is no human resources department, you have nothing to lose by asking, "Do you think one of your instructors would have time to talk with me for a minute or so?" If you're lucky enough to get through to a person who might be of help, go back to your original list of questions to see if you can generate some interest.

When you find someone willing to discuss possible employment, ask if you might send a résumé and a letter of introduction.

LETTERS

Treat any responses you receive to letters that lead to interviews as though you were interviewing for an open position, with the following exception: You are *creating* the opening, or at least interviewing for a position for which there is as yet no competition. This puts you in a more comfortable position than that of most job interviewees, but it doesn't mean that you can relax and not do your best in the interview.

NEWSPAPER WANT ADS

Responding to newspaper ads can be frustrating, because often there is no feedback after you've taken the time and effort to put together a résumé and cover letter. Still, there is always the possibility that an ad will lead to your next position, so once you accept it for the long shot it is, you can devote as much time as you need to responding to those ads that deserve it. A good way to keep your ad-answering campaign effective is to rate all of the ads under consideration as "1s," "2s," or "3s," against the following criteria:

It's a 1 if: The ad reads like your dream job, and is a mirror of your résumé.

Strategy: Respond as though you personally had been asked to interview for the position. Research the hiring organization extensively so that you can demonstrate in a cover letter knowledge of the employer that you couldn't get from reading the ad alone. Be sure your résumé Objective exactly reflects the title given for the open position. Edit your Summary to include all aspects of your background that match the employer's needs. Write a cover letter that answers the ad's requirements point for point, in the same sequence they were printed. Write—and then rewrite—a description of those accomplishments, skills, and responsibilities that relate specifically to each requirement, and then streamline it by deleting all excess words.

It's a 2 if: The job is a near match. You know you can easily satisfy four of the five or so requirements specified for the position. In short, you know you can do the job.

Strategy: Give the letter at least an hour of your time, checking off those of your accomplishments and skills that match up with the stated requirements. Stress your advertisement-related strengths, and don't even mention the one or two credentials you may lack.

It's a 3 if: The job sounds good. It may be a stretch for you the way it is described, but you're pretty sure you could handle it.

Strategy: Give it a "short-term best shot": your résumé accompanied by a letter stating your qualifications as powerfully as you can. But don't spend a lot of time on it; there are probably a large number of applicants ahead of you.

There is also a fourth rating for newspaper ads worth mentioning. Often an ad will suggest to you additional jobs that may open up after the first position is filled. Say you're looking for aerobics instructor openings, and you see an ad for a director or assistant director at a local health club. As soon as that position is filled, it may well create the need for additional staff, including, presumably, one or more aerobics instructors. If such an opportunity suggests itself and you believe you would be a good candidate for such a position, put the ad in a "suspense" file for further reference. Call periodically to see if the job has been filled and by whom, and ask for an interview when you get through to the right person. The downside: Filling the first job may take several months before candidates are considered for jobs generated by it.

EMPLOYMENT AGENCIES

The truth is, not many entry-level jobs are filled through employment agencies. With this in mind, it still is not a bad idea to find out which agencies in your immediate area (or the nearest larger metropolitan area) list the most jobs in sports, fitness, and recreation from day to day and week to week. Just don't rely heavily on them. Call, make an appointment to personally give your résumé to one of the counselors, and then move on.

Call a counselor at each of those that have recently listed sports, fitness, and recreation jobs, even if your specialty is not among them. Be prepared to rework your résumé if the counselor thinks it will help to match you more closely with a specific assignment.

Employment agencies work for client employers first, because that is where their fees come from, so don't expect a lot of career counseling. If a counselor believes your background will lead to a placement, however, you'll get more than just passing attention. This is not because these are thoughtless people, but because in their business they usually don't have the time to both counsel you and earn a living for themselves. In response to direct questions, the good counselors usually are willing to offer tips you can use. Just don't expect them to spend a lot of time with you.

Be sure to arrange at least one personal interview at each agency. Try to present yourself as a cooperative, qualified candidate, not just a body with a résumé. This will improve your chances.

Call each counselor every few weeks or so, not so often as to become a nuisance, but often enough to both be kept in mind and stay on top of any trends that may be developing. Though your odds of getting a job through an agency are high, it is only common sense to spread your name around as widely as possible. Each call will take just a minute or two out of your day, and who knows—you may just remind a disorganized counselor that there's an opportunity out there for which you would match nicely and, not incidentally, generate a fee from the employer client.

TRADE PUBLICATION ARTICLES AND CLASSIFIEDS

Spend a half day every week at the best public or college library available to you to scan those trade magazines that may contain information on trends in your specialty that may affect your marketing strategy. Such magazines as *American Fitness, Club Industry,* and *Personal Trainer*, for example, carry articles that will help you to learn more about the field, as well as what some of its leaders think, and what they see as ways to improve the occupation's effectiveness and future. Identify contact people and examine any classified ads for openings of interest to you. A good source directory for sports, fitness, and recreation trade magazines is *Magazine Industry Marketplace*, revised annually and available at most libraries' reference desks. (*Note*: Because most of these magazines are published for national distribution, read them for job leads only if you are prepared to relocate, or you live in a major metropolitan area.)

DATABASE SERVICES

Most public libraries also use one or more of a number of database services offered by a growing number of providers. Again, the larger the city you live in or near, the more effective these services will be to you. Here are five of the most popular:

- **Infotrac:** A journal and newspaper article index providing data about prospective employers

- **Business Dateline OnDisc:** Business articles appearing in local, state, and regional journals, newspapers, and magazines that are of interest to job seekers

- **ProQuest:** Business articles in newspapers and magazines

- **Standard & Poor's Corporation:** Listings of public and private companies as well as biographical listings

- **Ultimate Job Finder:** 4,500 sources of trade and specialty journals

USEFUL WEB SITES

- **InfoTrac Web**
  http://www.infotrac.galegroup.com

- **Business Dateline**
  http://www.lib.usm.edu/~libinfo/databases/bizdate.html

- **Career Exploration Links**
  http://www.uhs.berkeley.edu/CareerLibrary/links/careerme.htm

- **Career Guides: Jobsmart**
  http://jobsmart.org/tools/career/spec-car.htm

- **Career Builder**
  http://www.careerbuilder.com

PROFESSIONAL NETWORKS

We mentioned in Chapter One that when you select a specialty there will be at least one professional organization available to help you keep up with trends and assure that your professional interests are being looked after, on a number of levels. For many trade associations, making members aware of employment opportunities is a substantial part of the benefit of belonging. Refer to your specialty chapter to find out how to contact the organization most likely to post job openings, either nationally or, more specifically, by state or region. A list of all of the specialty professional organizations mentioned in the book is provided as a separate resource in Appendix A.

INTERNET JOB BANKS AND JOB SITES

If you are a stranger to on-line and Internet sources as part of your job-search strategy, you are missing more than you realize. If you do not have a computer, ask your high school guidance counselor what services exist at school, and if tutoring might be arranged for you. If your school does not have such services, go to the nearest large public library. Most have one or more computers available for public use, and there is usually a librarian on staff to assist interested students and adults.

If a computer is available but you are not familiar with on-line job search, one way to make up for this is to visit a local bookstore. Take time to examine all books on the topic before putting any money down. Two to consider are *The Complete Idiot's Guide to the Internet*, by Peter Kent, and *Dern's Internet Guide for New Users*, by Daniel Dern.

Here's a sad truth to keep in mind after you've gotten this far: The vast majority of job openings to be found on the Internet are directed toward experienced workers. Not too much exists for the first-time job seeker.

Still, for those of you who intend to move upward in your field and who want to know what requirements are expected for, say, the job your boss has, as well as where such jobs are and what they pay, this is an excellent source for you.

Your first stop should be *http://www.sportsworld.com*, where more than 100 Canadian and U.S. jobs will be listed at any one time, all of which remain posted for 90 days.

Most of the existing commercial on-line services (CompuServe, America Online, and Prodigy are three) offer networking opportunities and job-search capabilities, but this is a much more effective avenue for experienced job seekers than for those just out of high school. It is also more effective for those who live in big city markets—or who are willing to move to one—where the greatest number of jobs are likely to be.

Even so, through their interactive special interest areas—called "forums," "bulletin boards," or "newsgroups," depending on the service—you can some-times zero in on your specialty, introduce yourself, state your objective, and wait for the responses to come in. Make a list of the sites on which you have made inquiries, and check them at least twice a week.

Most of the leading job-search sites, similarly, are likely to be of little help. On a recent visit to one of them, Monster.com. (*www.monster.com*), we saw 466,182 jobs advertised in the United States. We clicked on "Search Jobs" among the home page options, which led to a page containing two boxes to further narrow the search: In the first it is possible to scroll through nearly

250 U.S. locations; in the second you can click on one or more of the 43 vocational categories listed, among them "Sports and Recreation." Testing approximately 35 sites, we found 6 jobs listed for Los Angeles (Lifeguard, Personal Trainer, Aquatics Director, Group Exercise Instructor, Sports Marketing Intern, and Marketing/Promotions Intern); 3 for Philadelphia; and 15 in Salt Lake City, all related to the 2002 Winter Olympics to be held there. Most of the others had either a single opening or no jobs at all.

Still, it won't hurt for you to check "Sports and Recreation" jobs from time to time in the states and cities that interest you.

Neither CompuServe nor America Online listed a single sports, fitness, or recreation job. The pickings, therefore, are likely to be slim; at least they were on the last day we were able to check before this book went to press. Still, it takes only a few minutes to find out, and you might have much better luck by the time this book is available.

A FEW KEY POINTS TO REMEMBER

• Most first-time permanent job seekers will have the best luck finding a job through newspaper ads, personnel agencies, or word of mouth.

• For job seekers changing careers, relying only on personnel agencies and newspaper ads eliminates at least half of the prospective employers.

• Specialty publication articles and ads, database services, direct proposals, professional networks, and Internet job banks are all excellent potential sources for jobs.

CHAPTER NINE

How to Interview Effectively

What is the secret to developing an interview strategy that generates job offers? One word: preparation.

The more knowledgeable you are about your prospective employers, the easier it will be for them to visualize you as a valued employee. But first, they want to see if you can solve whatever problems might be keeping them from providing the best service or product in the most cost-effective manner.

KNOW YOUR PROSPECTIVE EMPLOYERS

Even though you may be applying for an entry-level job, you need to learn as much as you can about the employer before the interview, including the job you are interviewing for and your prospective boss. You can go about this in several ways, depending on how you found out about the position in the first place: from an agency, through an advertisement, or by networking, either on or off the Internet.

If you answered an ad and the employer was named, there are several ways you can gather information about it. For instance, publicly held large Health and Fitness clubs, such as Bally Total Fitness Corporation, are required by law to report various kinds of data, all of which are available to the public in a number of business directories. Some of these directories specialize by industry, others by size. In general, more data are available about the larger, publicly held companies, although Dun & Bradstreet's *Million Dollar Directory* lists the top 50,000 companies with a net worth of more than $500,000. Increasing numbers of companies provide information on the Internet, as well, through home pages in several business-oriented databases.

One of the most informative of these sources is the *Directory of Corporate Affiliations*, which is published annually and updated with bimonthly supplements. An index in an accompanying volume lists more than 40,000 divisions, subsidiaries, affiliates, and parent companies, and the page on which the complete listing of each appears. This is followed by extensive data for the 4,000 parent companies, including address, telephone number, stock exchange or exchanges, approximate annual sales, number of employees, type of business, and top corporate officers. It also lists all divisions, subsidiaries, affiliates, and so on, with address, telephone number, type of business, and name of chief operating officer.

Additional geographical and Standard Industrial Classification (S.I.C.) indexes list all companies by city and state, and primary types of business, respectively. The *Directory of Corporate Affiliations* is one of the few commercial reference works that keeps up with the growing whirlwind of acquisitions and mergers. (*Tip*: Check S.I.C.s 0910–0980 for fishing and hunting; 4400–4500 for water transportation; 4700–4800 for transportation services such as tour operators; 5088–5091 for transportation, sporting, and recreational goods and supplies; 5941 for sporting goods and bicycle shops; 7000–8000 for miscellaneous recreation outlets, such as physical fitness facilities, golf courses, bowling alleys, and professional sports clubs.) If you think other occupations may interest you, spend a few minutes to look through the entire list of Standard Industrial Classifications.

Other general interest and industry-specific directories to consult are:

Business Organizations, Agencies, and Publications Directory
Corporate 1000
Directories in Print (Volumes I and II)
Dun's Million Dollar Directory (Volumes I, II, and III)
Encyclopedia of Business Information Sources
International Corporate 1000
Macmillan Directory of Leading Private Companies
Small Business Sourcebook
Standard Directory of Advertisers

Other directories are available, perhaps including your career specialty. Ask your school or public librarian for help, or for other suggestions. You might start with *Directories in Print*, published semiannually, which is exactly what it says it is.

But no matter where you get your information or how small the prospective employer, it is to your advantage to go into an interview knowing the full range of an employer's services.

Other good sources are neighbors, family members, or friends who may know somebody at a managerial or executive level at the company or facility that interests you. By asking further you may be able to learn the name of the person hiring for the position, and something about his or her background.

Finally, go back over the ad that got you the interview in the first place. Memorize every word of every requirement. Your answers should all be framed by what you know the employer is looking for. Here's an exercise to help you prepare:

PREPARING FOR YOUR INTERVIEW

Whether your interview was set up by an employment agency, or as a result of your answering an ad or networking your way into a contact, the first part of your preparation should be focused on the institution itself. Answer as many questions as you can from the list below:

What position does the employer want to fill?

_____

_____

_____

What attracted you to the job?

_____

_____

_____

What academic background or special courses are required?

_____

_____

_____

What are the skills needed for the job? (For example, working well under pressure, problem solving, initiative, ability to work with any special equipment.)

_____

_____

_____

For each of the skills you have identified, list specific examples of instances in which you have demonstrated that skill. (Space is provided for four skills.)

1. _____

    _____

    _____

2. _____

    _____

    _____

3. _____

    _____

    _____

4. _____

    _____

    _____

USING AN EMPLOYMENT AGENCY

If you are working with an effective employment agency counselor, you have little to worry about. Because they live by the client fees generated by the people they place, agency professionals will work harder if they sense that you may be one of their next placements. They will coach you to say everything they think will benefit you in the interview. Some counselors are more efficient than others, however. And it is those "others" who can hurt you if you don't take matters into your own hands.

Here are some kinds of data you will find extremely helpful as you prepare for the interview. If your agency counselor has not already supplied you with the following kinds of information, ask for it. (*Note*: The following categories assume a health club setting. Adapt them as necessary for the type of institution to which you are applying.)

1. Employer
   - Customer volume (this year; last two years)

   - Number of employees

   - Growth prospects; strengths and weaknesses

   - Possible problems (why they exist; how they might be overcome)

2. Position
   - Why is it open? (When was it last open, and why?)

   - How long has it been open? (If two months or more, why so tough to fill?)

   - Where is the person who previously held it? (Can we talk to him or her?)

   - How many people have been interviewed so far?

   - Where are they in the hiring process? (How many candidates are still in the running? Why are they still being considered?)

   - What are the prospects for advancement?

   - What do you think will be the determining factor in getting the job?

- Why do you think I am still a candidate? (What do they like about me?)

- How many others are doing the same work?

- What is the salary policy? How are raises determined? How good is the benefits program?

- How will performance be measured?

3. Boss
   - Title?

   - Background? Previous experience?

   - How long with this company?

   - Do you know him or her personally, or have you talked only with human resources?

   - What are his or her prospects with the health club?

NETWORKING AND RESEARCH LEADS

If you have researched a position that interests you and have written a good enough letter and résumé to be rewarded with an interview, ask the person you heard from what the focus of your meeting will be so you can prepare adequately. (Will you be interviewing for a specific position, for example? Does an opening exist?) Then attempt to get as much of the information listed in the preceding section to help you get a handle on employer, position, and prospective boss.

THE FIRST INTERVIEW

Here's the worst news first: The job does not always go to the most qualified candidate. Even though most human resource interviewers are skilled at their jobs and usually recommend those candidates who fulfill the initial requirements for an open position, direct supervisors themselves often lack good interviewing skills. On what basis, then, are many hiring decisions made? The answer: first impressions.

FIRST IMPRESSIONS

Given two or more candidates with similar backgrounds, the job will almost invariably go to the person who projects the most honesty, sincerity, and enthusiasm. Those of you who want to work in a bicycle or ski shop, where considerable on-duty time is spent in direct customer or public contact, will be judged on the empathy and compassion you project as well. Other personal qualities that count more than they should are physical appearance, mannerisms, vocabulary, attitude, and nonverbal communication.

Your feeling of confidence can profoundly affect a first impression. That confidence, in turn, can be generated initially by something as fundamental as sound preparation. Don't underestimate it. Your confidence level will lead to an attitude that the employer needs you, rather than the other way around. *Feel* successful and chances are better that you will *be* successful; it becomes a self-fulfilling prophecy.

Before the interview, go over the résumé you have provided the interviewer. (If you have written more than one version, be sure to have the differences straight in your head.) Treat every résumé entry as if it were a script cue. You were brought in for an interview in the first place because your background was of interest. If you have been able to find out exactly what aspects of your background they like, that puts you ahead of the game. One way to determine this is to go over your résumé line by line. Think of responses to questions that will allow you to elaborate on your accomplishments; for example, the interviewer may ask:

"So you were a lifeguard during the summer between your junior and senior years. What would you say are the most important things you learned that summer?"

This gives you the opportunity to go into as much detail as you need to relate the duties you held in this summer job to those for which you would be responsible in the job under discussion.

First interviews should be viewed as one-shot opportunities. As such, rehearse all résumé-entry elaborations as though this will be the only chance you have to tell your story. Actually, that may well be the case. Be prepared to speak for ten seconds to a minute or more about any given résumé entry, depending on where the interviewer's interest lies.

Here is a good way to get this done:

PREPARING TO ANSWER RÉSUMÉ QUESTIONS

Keeping in mind the requirements for the job and what you believe the employer is looking for, use your résumé to prepare a discussion of your accomplishments. In the left-hand column, list all accomplishments mentioned on your résumé. In the right-hand column, explain why and how you attained them.

Accomplishments   Why and How Attained

1. _____   _____
   _____   _____
   _____   _____

2. _____   _____
   _____   _____
   _____   _____

3. _____   _____
   _____   _____
   _____   _____

4. _____   _____
   _____   _____
   _____   _____

5. _____   _____

   _____   _____

   _____   _____

RESPONDING TO TOUGH QUESTIONS

Though every interview is different, all will include one or more questions that you would just as soon not have to answer. The interviewer will be listening not only for content but also for sincerity, poise, and an ability to think quickly. Spend some time before your interview developing answers to questions you think might give you trouble. Some of them may be tough and fair; some of them may be tough and unfair.

If you were fired from a summer or part-time job, this will undoubtedly come up at the interview. Answer all questions truthfully, but without excessive detail. If you were fired because your performance or attitude was in question, emphasize the ways you have made this a learning experience, as well as the extent to which you have profited from it. Try to anticipate additional questions intended to get more details about your termination, and rehearse your answers repeatedly.

This is a key stage of the interview. If you can get beyond this early mine field, you will be able to concentrate on more positive and productive matters.

Most interviewers ask one or more tough questions. Some interviewers seem to ask nothing but tough questions. Basically, they simply want to know what you can offer them and catalog your strengths and weaknesses. After writing answers to the questions that follow, memorize and rehearse them.

What do you know about us? (Do the research so you will have some key information.)

_____

_____

_____

Why do you want to work for us? (Words and phrases to think about in formulating your answer: challenge; industry leader; quality of product; growth potential.)

_____

_____

_____

What would you do for us? What can you do for us that someone else can't? (Relate your answer in terms of the employer's needs.)

_____

_____

_____

Why should we hire you? (Not because you "need a job." Think about specific contributions you can make.)

_____

_____

_____

What are your strong points?

_____

_____

_____

What are your weak points? (No one is perfect. The trick is to identify weaknesses you are aware of that you are attempting to eliminate.)

_____

_____

_____

As difficult as this may sound, you'll do the best job if you try to view the interview as a meeting between two equals—you're the "seller"; the interviewer is the "buyer"—to explore what each has to offer the other. If you have something the employer wants, that equal feeling will be established in a hurry. Listen to the questions behind the questions; for example:

"Who was your best boss? Describe him (or her)." (In what kind of working environment is this person most comfortable? What tendencies might there be regarding loyalty, self-starting, or working independently?)

ASKING YOUR OWN QUESTIONS

Don't feel you must wait until the end of the interview to ask questions of your own. Think of every possible aspect of the job you want to know about, every aspect of the target employer you want to know about, and every aspect of your prospective boss's background and management style you want to know about. Have your questions prepared accordingly. At appropriate times during the interview, answer the question directed at you and follow up with a question of your own on the same topic; for example:

"So sure, I'd be willing to work overtime taking inventory when you need it done. By the way, are there other kinds of work I might be trained to do after I become familiar with the way things operate here?"

INTERVIEW WRAP-UP

Much can depend on how you perform toward the end of the interview. Remember, this is your last opportunity to nail down the job offer, if you think you are getting close. It's an opportunity to make sure you get invited back for a second interview, if an offer is not made that day. It's also a chance to resurrect your candidacy if you think an earlier, hastily worded answer has damaged you.

When you feel that the interview is coming to a close ("Any further questions?" "Well, I guess that covers just about everything"), go out in as strong a position as you can. This is your chance to ask all of the questions you were not able to ask earlier. The response to one of them, if you have not established it previously, should include a clear awareness of the kind of person the employer is looking for.

If you still want the job as badly as you did at the start of the interview, ask for it. Restate your understanding of the requirements, and your ability to meet them. Then sum up; for example, "I'd just like you to know, Ms. Jones, that I'm very interested in this position. I also believe it is a job that I can do well."

Ask a final question designed to assess or crystallize your candidacy. ("Where do you think we stand?" "What's the next step?" "How soon will you be making a decision?")

At this point you have done all you can do. Thank the interviewer for his or her time, and leave.

You have two final responsibilities after you leave the interview. The first is to find a quiet corner and record your impressions, as completely as possible. Describe any additional job requirements that came to light during the interview, as well as the extent to which you conveyed your ability to perform them. Jot down all other information that was new to you, plus any changes, for better or worse, that altered your perspective of the opportunity. Finally, write down all job-related questions yet to be answered.

Your second responsibility is to write a follow-up letter to the interviewer as a way of (1) indicating your continued interest, (2) offering any additional reasons for you to be hired, and (3) resurrecting any "soft spots" in the interview to correct a misimpression.

An alternative, if you feel comfortable with it, is to follow up with a phone call. This can be more effective than a letter, but it is considerably more risky because it presupposes your ability to think quickly and to field any additional off-the-wall questions to the interviewer's satisfaction.

THE SECOND INTERVIEW

Your invitation for a second interview means that you have impressed the employer with your ability to do the job. Your competition probably has been narrowed down to anywhere from one to five other candidates. Presumably you have a good enough reading by this time of your prospective boss's personality and way of viewing the job to know how to elevate your candidacy and give yourself the best chance of getting the job offer.

Think of the things that got you this far in the first place and seemed to make the most favorable impact. Conversely, try to think of reasons you weren't offered the job immediately after the first interview.

Prepare for your second interview as follows: After reviewing your notes from the first interview, make two three-column charts, one for your job-related Assets, and one for your Liabilities. In Column A of your Assets chart, record all of your qualifications for the job. In Column B, assess your success in getting across each qualification to the interviewer. In Column C, list the extent to which you must restate each qualification, perhaps by describing a specific accomplishment (in a sense, A minus B).

In the Liabilities chart, include those qualifications for the job that you do not have, along with other possible negatives to your candidacy. List these in Column A, by category. In Column B, record how well you handled these deficiencies in the first interview. In Column C, detail the work that yet needs to be done (again, A minus B). The tables will look like this:

ASSETS

Column A	Column B	Column C
My Qualifications	Extent Covered Previously	Points Yet to Be Made

LIABILITIES

Column A	Column B	Column C
Deficiencies/Liabilities	How Well Handled Previously	How I Will Overcome

Keep a sense of perspective as you work through your assets and liabilities, and the extent to which you need to deal with them in the second interview. The act of writing them down will by itself give you a clearer picture of where you stand. It may well be that this alone will help you remain on top of the situation, determining what issues are still a concern, and allowing you to deal with them in a straightforward, confident manner.

After doing your best to overcome whatever objections to your candidacy you think still remain, try to determine from the interviewer how successful you have been. Ask such questions as:

"Does that answer cover all of the ground you wanted it to?"

Or,

"Is there anything else you'd like me to add to that?"

Or,

"What more can I tell you?"

If the response to any of these summary questions is ambiguous or inconclusive, you have nothing to lose by testing the waters. A final question to the interviewer to see if you can learn what is delaying a job offer might be:

"Is there anything up to this point that leads you to believe I'm not the ideal candidate for the job?"

If you get a straight answer, at least you have something tangible to deal with, and the opportunity to neutralize the interviewer's objection. If not, you have the satisfaction of knowing you did all you could to get the job.*

TAKING YOUR NEW-JOB PULSE

Get in the habit of monitoring your performance, beginning your first day on the job. Don't just keep track of successful assignments; evaluate your relationships with the people around you: subordinates, peers, and supervisors. Learn to assess your ability and willingness to anticipate and solve those problems within your sphere of influence. Also:

---

* Parts of this section were adapted from *Conquer Interview Objections*, by Robert F. Wilson and Erik H. Rambusch. New York: John Wiley & Sons, 1994.

- Ask for feedback. Colleagues you trust see things you do not. Find a time to occasionally ask your boss, "How am I doing?" well before your performance review, so if corrective action is indicated, you can do what you have to do.

- Record your accomplishments. Make a copy of every good report that led to a solved problem, departmental or institutional growth, or reduced expenses.

- Spread your wings. Broaden and enrich your professional reputation by getting involved in your specialty's state, regional, and national organizations. Become active; volunteer for assignments at workshops, seminars, and meetings.

- Look for opportunities. After a year or two on your new job, an opening may occur elsewhere in the organization more consistent with your talents and long-term career goals. *Follow organizational procedure to the letter* (to be sure your ambition is not interpreted as dissatisfaction with your current assignment—or your boss!). Then use the interviewing skills learned in this book to improve your chances.

Treat the new opportunity as you would an opening elsewhere. Many fail to realize they may be competing with excellent candidates outside the organization or facility, and proceed as though their performance record and inside status automatically give them a decisive edge. They do not. Those who realize this have the best chance for success.

Good luck with your job search, and with the new job you find as a result.

A FEW KEY POINTS TO REMEMBER

- Before an interview, learn as much as you can about the job and your prospective boss.
- To prepare for your interview, memorize your résumé as you would a script, to be ready for all résumé-related questions.
- Write a follow-up letter to your interviewer after every interview.

Appendices

Advantage International
1025 Thomas Jefferson Street N.W.
Washington, DC 20007
(202)333-3838

Aerobic Pipeline International
3617 Drakeshire Drive
Modesto, CA 95356
(209)576-2611

Aerobics and Fitness Association of America
(AFAA)
15250 Ventura Boulevard, Suite 200
Sherman Oaks, CA 91403
(1-800)446-AFAA

African-American Association of Fitness
Professionals (AAAFP)
1507 E. 53rd Street, Suite 495
Chicago, IL 60615
(773)854-5842

American Academy of Health and Fitness
Professionals (AAHFP)
333 Estudillo Avenue, Suite A
San Leandro, CA 94577
(1-800)572-2237
Web:http://www.aahfp.com

American Association for Active Lifestyles and
Fitness (AAALF)
1900 Association Drive
Reston, VA 20191-1599
(1-800)213-7193
Web:http://www.aahperd.org/aaalf/aaalf.html

American Council on Exercise (ACE)
5820 Oberling Drive, Suite 102
San Diego, CA 92121
(1-800)825-3636

American Fitness Professionals and Associates
(AFPA)
P.O. Box 214
Ship Bottom, NJ 08008
(1-800)494-7782
Web:http://www.AFPAfitness.com

American Senior Fitness Association (ASFA)
P.O. Box 2575
New Smyrna Beach, FL 32170
(1-800)243-1478, (904)423-6634

Aquatic Alliance International (AAI)
59 Prospect St, #2
Lebanon, NH 03766
Web:http://www.mindspring.com/~aai_getwet

Aquatic Exercise Association (AEA)
P.O. Box 1609
Nokomis, FL 34274-1609
(1-888)AEA-WAVE
Web:http://www.aeawave.com

Association for Worksite Health Promotion
(AWHP)
60 Revere Drive, Suite 500
Northbrook, IL 60062
(847)480-9574
Web:http://www.awhp.com

Athletic Equipment Managers Association
6224 Hester Road
Oxford, OH 45056
(513)523-2362

Baylor Sports Medicine Institute
P.O. Box 130258
Houston, TX 77219
(1-800)899-7348
Web:*http://www.bcm.tmc.edu/ortho/bsmi/
educate.htm*

Brinkman-Froemming Umpire School
1021 Indian River Drive
Cocoa, FL 32922
(407)639-1515

CAT Sports
5966 La Place Court
Carlsbad, CA 92008
(619)438-8080

Corporate Fitness Works, Inc.
18558 Office Park Drive
Montgomery Village, MD 20886
Web:*http://corporatefitnessworks.com*

ECA World Fitness Alliance
64 Franklin Boulevard
Long Beach, NY 11561
(516)432-6877
Web:*http://www.ecaworldfitness.com*

FACT: Fitness Awareness CEC Training Inc.
3330 Dundee Road, Suite N-4
Northbrook, IL 60062
(1-800)876-FACT

Golden Bear Sports Management
11780 U.S. Highway One
North Palm Beach, FL 33408
(407)626-3900

Golf Course Superintendents Association of
America
1421 Research Park Drive
Lawrence, Kansas 66049
(913)841-2240

Harry Wendelstedt School for Umpiring
88 South St. Andrews Drive
Ormond Beach, FL 32174
(904)672-4879

IDEA
6190 Cornerstone Court East, Suite 204
San Diego, CA 92121-3773
(1-800)999-4332, ext.7
Web:*http://www.ideafit.com*

International Association of Auditorium
Managers
4425 West Airport Freeway
Irving, TX 75062
(214)255-8020

International Fitness Professionals Association
(IFPA)
P.O. Box 6008
Palm Harbor, FL 34684
(1-800)785-1924
Web:*http://www.ifpa-fitness.com*

International Health, Racquet & Sportsclub
Association (IHRSA)
263 Summer Street
Boston, MA 02210
(1-800)228-4772
Web:*http://www.ihrsa.org*

International Sports Sciences Association
(ISSA)
3920-B State Street
Santa Barbara, CA 93105
(1-800)892-4772
Web:*http://www.issaonline.com*

International Weightlifting Association (IWA)
P.O. Box 444
Hudson, OH 44236-9347
(1-800) WEIGHTS

Jim Evans' Academy of Professional Umpiring
12885 Research Boulevard
Austin, TX 78750
(512)335-5959

National Association for Fitness Certification
(NAFC)
P.O. Box 67
Sierra Vista, AZ 85636
(1-800)324-8315
Web:*http://www.theriver.com/bodybasics*

National Association of Sports Officials
2017 Lathrop Avenue
Racine, WI 53405
(414)632-8855

National Athletic Trainers' Association (NATA)
2952 Stemmons Freeway
Dallas, TX 75247
Web:*http://www.nata.org*

National Basketball Referees Association
P.O. Box 3522
Santa Monica, California 90408
(310)393-3522

National Federation of Interscholastic Officials
Association
11724 Plaza Circle
Kansas City, MO 64195
(816)464-5400

National Federation of Professional Trainers
(NFPT)
P.O. Box 4579
Lafayette, IN 47903
(1-800) SAY-NFPT
Web:*http://www.nfpt.com*

National Institute for Fitness and Sport (NIFS)
250 University Boulevard
Indianapolis, IN 46202
(317)274-3432

National Operating Committee on Standards
for Athletic Equipment
P.O. Box 12290
Overland Park, KS 66282

National Strength and Conditioning
Association (NSCA)
P.O. Box 38909
Colorado Springs, CO 80937
(719)632-6722
Web:*http://www.nsca-lift.org*

Pro-Serv
1101 Wilson Boulevard
Arlington, VA 22209
(703)276-3030

Public Relations Society of America
33 Irving Place
New York, NY 10003
(212)995-2230

Sport Marketing Quarterly
P.O. Box 4425
Morgantown, WV 26504
(304)599-3482

Sports Turf Managers Association
P.O. Box 809119
Chicago, Illinois 60680
(312)644-6610

Stadium Managers Association
875 Kings Highway
Woodbury, NJ 08096
(609)384-6287

Umpire Development Office
201 Bayshore Drive S.E.
St. Petersburg, Florida 33731
(813)823-1286

World Instructor Training Schools
S.F. & Wellness Inc.
206 76th, Suite A
Virginia Beach, VA 23451
(1-888)330-WITS
Web:*http://witseducation.com*

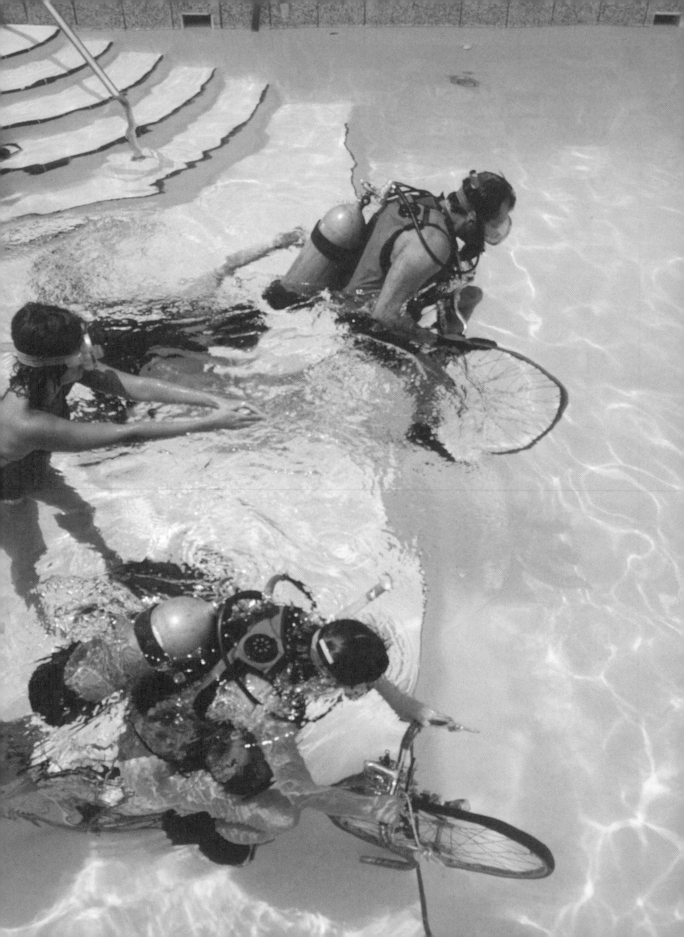

Sports, Fitness, and Recreation Sources

Fisher, David, *The 50 Coolest Jobs in Sports*. New York: Macmillan USA, 1997. How to get a job in the exciting world of sports, even if you weren't a medal winner. Provides profiles that give job responsibilities, training and education requirements, and salary ranges.

Harkavy, Michael, *101 Careers: A Guide to the Fastest-Growing Opportunities*. New York: John Wiley & Sons, Inc., 1990. Not much here on specific sports and fitness occupations, but a good overview of sales and marketing if that's your interest.

Heitzmann, William Ray, *Careers for Sport Nuts and Other Athletic Types* (Second Edition). Lincolnwood, IL: NTC/Contemporary Publishing Company, 1997. How to get started turning your passion for sports into a rewarding profession.

Miller, Mary, *Opportunities in Fitness Careers*, Lincolnwood, IL: NTC/Contemporary Publishing Company, 1997. A good overview of careers in the health fitness field, with information on educational requirements, salary projections, and advice on finding materials on-line.

Occupational Outlook Handbook, 2000–2001 Edition. Washington, D.C.: U.S. Department of Labor, Bureau of Labor Statistics, 2000. A nationally recognized source of career information for nearly 50 years. Describes what workers do on the job, the training and education needed, earnings, working conditions, and job prospects. Some good information on the recreation field.

Job-Search Books and Videos

Criscito, Pat, *Designing the Perfect Résumé*. Hauppauge, NY: Barron's Educational Series, Inc., 1995. How to use a home computer to design a professional-looking résumé. Hundreds of samples created with WordPerfect software. Includes practical details such as effective use of layout, section heads, type fonts, bullets, and graphic devices. Tips on designing effective letterheads and cover letters, as well.

Crowther, Karmen, *Researching Your Way to a Good Job*. New York: John Wiley & Sons, Inc., 1993. Provides tools and techniques to examine potential employers and jobs, and job-related information on other communities, if you intend to relocate.

Dern, Daniel P., *Dern's Internet Guide for New Users*. New York: McGraw-Hill, Inc., 1998. Written in an informal style; features segments such as Quick Tips, Try This, Internet

Humor, and What the Experts Say. The jumpstart section for true beginners includes the Net Buddy System.

Internet Yellow Pages, 1996 Edition. Berkeley, CA: Osborne/McGraw-Hill. A user-friendly guide to the Internet. Several pages related to healthcare, including newsgroups, information, discussion clubs, research, etc. Good networking source.

Strunk, William, Jr., and E.B. White, *Elements of Style* (Third Edition). New York: Macmillan Publishing Co., Inc., 1979. When you're constructing résumés and cover letters, there's no better little book in print to help you make every word count.

Wilson, Robert F., *Interview to Win Your First Job* (Third Edition). Saxtons River, VT: Wilson Mcleran, Inc., 2000. Video and workbook program for high school and college students preparing for their first full-time, permanent job search.

Scholarship, Grant, and Low-Cost Loan Sources

Need a Lift. The American Legion. Details on the various programs this veterans' organization sponsors on behalf of needy students. (Similar programs available from such civic groups as the YMCA, 4-H Club, Elks, Kiwanis, Jaycees, Chamber of Commerce, Girl Scouts, and Boy Scouts. Contact your local chapter or office for further information.)

Paying Less for College. Princeton, NJ: Peterson's Guides, 1995. Comprehensive guide to the more than $36 billion awarded annually in institutional, private, state, and federal aid. Sixteen hundred-plus college financial aid profiles and cost comparisons "not found elsewhere," reads the back-cover blurb. Explains new financial aid application process. Indexes of colleges offering scholarships for athletics, academics, civic or religious service, and ethnic and religious background.

Schlachter, Gail Ann, and R. David Weber, *Directory of Financial Aid for Afro-Americans, 1995–1997*. San Carlos, CA: References Services Press. Contains more than 500 sources: government agencies, private organizations, corporations, sororities and fraternities, foundations, religious groups, and military and veterans' associations providing assistance, either exclusively or primarily for Afro-American students. The inside story on eligibility; number, amount, and kind of assistance awarded (and for how long); how, where, and when to apply; what limitations might be applicable. (Companion volumes are also available prepared specifically for Hispanic and Asian-American students.)

Student Guide to Federal Financial Aid Programs, 1999–2000. User-friendly handbook through the maze of government assistance to higher education. Begins by mentioning complementary and supplementary sources at state level, in addition to other public and private sources. Explanations of every available grant and loan (including loans to parents)—contingencies, qualifications, deadlines, special circumstances that may affect eligibility, payback schedules, and list of important terms and concepts to understand. For a free copy, write Federal Student Aid Information Center, P.O. Box 84, Washington, D.C. 20044; or call (800)433-3243. (The student guide is also available on-line, on the Department of Education's web site, through the Internet. The site address is: *http://www.ed.gov.*)

YMCA Scholarships and Grants for Education and Training. YMCA of the USA, Leadership Development Group, 2000. Describes more than 20 scholarship assistance and grant programs created specifically to assist current and prospective YMCA staff members in the completion of undergraduate and graduate degrees required for successful YMCA careers.

Index